grief
five sequences

grief
five sequences

PROSE POEMS BY
Cassandra Atherton
Oz Hardwick
Paul Hetherington
Paul Munden
Jen Webb

authorised theft

grief: five sequences

authorised theft / Recent Work Press
Canberra, Australia

This chapbook series was produced with the support of International Poetry Studies (IPSI), based within the Centre for Creative and Cultural Research, Faculty of Arts and Design, University of Canberra.

Collection © Recent Work Press 2025

The copyright of the individual poems remains with the authors.

ISBN 978-1-7641068-2-5

Cover and page design: Caren Florance

RECENT WORK PRESS
2015-2025
10 YEARS OF POETRY

recentworkpress.com

CONTENTS

Introduction: *The Elusive Emotion* — vii
Research Background: *On Grief* — xi

Aegean Blues   Paul Hetherington — 1
Complicated   Oz Hardwick — 25
(O)bituary: The Little Deaths   Cassandra Atherton — 51
Modes of Mourning   Jen Webb — 77
Poems of 2024-25   Paul Munden — 103

Individual poets' statements — 129
About the poets — 144

The AUTHORISED THEFT series of poetry chapbooks was initiated by International Poetry Studies (IPSI) based in the Faculty of Arts and Design at the University of Canberra. The first collection of chapbooks – Cassandra Atherton's Pegs, *Paul Hetherington's* Jars, *Paul Munden's* Keys, *Jen Webb's* Gaps *and Jordan Williams'* Nets *– resulted from discussions connected to IPSI's Prose Poetry Project, inaugurated by IPSI in late 2014. A second collection,* The Taoist Elements, *followed in 2016; a third,* Colours, *in 2017; and a fourth,* Prosody, *in 2018. A fifth series,* The Six Senses, *followed in anthology form in 2019 and, in 2020, the sixth collection, also in anthology form, was entitled* C19: Intertext || Ekphrasis. *The 2021 anthology,* Five Ages, *took Hesiod's conceptualisation of human history as its starting point, including Oz Hardwick as a new contributing author, and in 2022, the anthology focused on the* Five Tastes, *and in 2023, the* Five Oceans. *This year's anthology,* Grief: Five Sequences, *is the tenth in the series. IPSI supports and promotes collaborative and collegiate poetic work in a variety of forms, and encourages the collaboration of poets with other artists, such as Caren Florance who has designed the series.*

INTRODUCTION

THE ELUSIVE EMOTION

PAUL HETHERINGTON

This volume's five groups of prose poems approach the subject of grief. I say 'approach' rather than 'address' because grief may not be a single, definable emotion – or, if it is, it may be considered 'overly complex' for ready analysis (Gustafson 1989: 457). The experience of grief often partakes of the ineffable and 'is a special case of emotion' (ibid.), partly because it manifests in a wide variety of ways. Additionally, in many experiences of grief, 'myriad symbolic losses and secondary losses occur that must also be grieved' (Koeppl 2004: 50).

Furthermore, various scholars understand contemporary poetry as fundamentally informed by grief. Jacqueline Kolosov remarks that 'Since 1900, or 1910 (the year Virginia Woolf said everything changed)' grief has become 'a continuous state of immersion' due to 'the cultural demise of faith and religious rituals associated with dying, industrialized warfare, mass genocide; and not least of all, the shutting away of the dying and the elderly in hospitals and nursing homes' (2012: 31).

Poetry about grief may approach the subject head-on, or slantwise through various forms of indirection. Or, the expression of the emotion may be deferred, to the extent that grief is not immediately recognisable in the writing. Given this, many poems that canvass issues other than grief are nevertheless, as it were, suffused with what one might call the ever-presence of it.

Grief has also been turned into a pathology by contemporary Western societies, even as the emotion so often fails to manifest in predictable ways, and many contemporary poems approach grief in this light. Linda Pastan's 'The Five Stages of Grief' is an example and part of the poem poignantly characterises the idea of denial:

> I sat down at breakfast
> carefully setting the table
> for two. I passed you the toast—
> you sat there. I passed
> you the paper—you hid
> behind it.   (1977: 128)

Grief can be hard to name. It may be slippery in the mind's fingers. And it may also be displaced into general ideas about human existence as a way of muting its agonising specificities. For instance, if a parent dies and is mourned, the associated grief may eventually be absorbed into the general recognition that parents eventually always die. Robyn L Ord recognises the ordinariness and prevalence of grief in remarking that in some cases 'grief does not need to be diagnosed, managed, or cured – for maybe the [grief-stricken] are just wandering, not needing to be found.' She also states, '[i]ndividuals grieve, cope with, and experience loss in many ways … Sometimes grief does not look the way we feel it should. Sometimes it is colourful' (2009: 207).

Meredith Martin might agree, having characterised grief in related terms:

> Grief has purple hair. Grief is absurd, jerking you around and making you think that maybe you are in control when you are absolutely not. It is preposterous, ridiculous, out of a cartoon or surreal dream.   (2024: 272)

Thus, while it is usually understood to be a serious subject, it is sometimes treated light-heartedly or humorously because of the recognition that serious approaches to grief do not always do full justice to its eddying, sometimes absurd-seeming complexities – that when it is 'preposterous, ridiculous' or like 'a cartoon or surreal dream' it may need to be represented in language that leavens the emotion's weight and ubiquity.

Grief is directly invoked, or lurks surreptitiously, in many works of literature. It is an overt preoccupation in some of these works and, in others, it is to some extent hidden or excluded, including by alternative themes and tropes. For example, Shakespeare's *Hamlet* is a play largely about the effects and consequences of grief, yet it is often considered notable for different preoccupations, and the Bell Shakespeare website lists the play's themes in this order: delay and inaction; moral corruption; masks, performing and theatre; gender; mortality; revenge; madness; doubles, divisions and reflections; and, finally, grief (n.d.: n.p.).

Early in the play, Hamlet speaks of grief directly, characterising it as a kind of touchstone for authentic feeling in a world full of complex dissembling: 'I have that within which passeth show;/ These but the trappings and the suits of woe' (1974: 873). Arthur Kirsch argues that Hamlet is:

> speaking of the early stages of grief, of its shock, of its inner and still hidden sense of loss, and trying to describe what is not fully describable – the literally inexpressible wound whose immediate consequence is the dislocation, if not transvaluation, of our customary perceptions and feelings and attachments to life.   (1981: 19)

As with this famous work, sometimes it seems that in literature and poetry, grief is almost everywhere one looks.

In this volume of prose poetry, Cassandra Atherton, Oz Hardwick, Paul Hetherington, Paul Munden and Jen Webb have approached grief in different ways. In their hands, the emotion is sometimes recognisable and sometimes disguised; and it is sometimes directly understood and often obliquely registered. Their works grieve for those who are gone while they traverse the idea of the abiding presence of loss. If a melancholy sense of absence is occasionally registered in these works, there is humour too. And, more generally, there are many salutary expressions of grief-inflected yet powerfully present feelings of love and desire.

Works Cited

Gustafson, Donald 1989 'Grief', *Noûs* 23.4: 457-79

'Hamlet: Themes', n.d. Bell Shakespeare website, n.p. https://www.bellshakespeare.com.au/hamlet-themes

Kirsch, Arthur 1981 'Hamlet's Grief', *ELH* 48.1: 17-36

Koeppl, Judith F 2004 'Grief', *GPSolo* 21.7: 50-51

Kolosov, Jacqueline 2012 'The Art of Losing: Four Contemporary American Women Poets and Grief', *The American Poetry Review* 41.6: 31-36

Martin, Meredith 2024 'Grief', *Paideuma: Modern and Contemporary Poetry and Poetics* 50: 271-72

Ord, Robyn L 2009 '"It's Like a Tattoo": Rethinking Dominant Discourses on Grief', *Canadian Social Work Review/Revue canadienne de service social* 26.2: 195-211

Pastan, Linda 1977 'Five Stages of Grief', *Chicago Review* 28.4: 128-29

Shakespeare, William 1974 *Hamlet*, in *The Complete Works of William Shakespeare* (ed WJ Craig), London: Oxford University Press, 870-907

RESEARCH BACKGROUND

ON GRIEF

JEN WEBB

Virtually every writer in history seems to have written something about grief. The first known poem that addresses the topic was written by the Sumerian priestess Enheduanna (c.2285 to 2250 BCE), who is herself the first known author. Her poem, the 'Exaltation of Inanna', recounts her pain and grief after she was driven into exile following an uprising in Ur; it includes her plea to the goddess Inanna for help and consolation, and her relief at the restoration to her home and her temple. The key point, though, is how she expresses the importance of writing in such circumstances: 'With "It is enough for me, it is too much for me!" I have given birth, oh exalted lady, (to this song) for you' (Hallo & van Dijk 1968: 138). *Enough for me; too much for me*: this is the creative process; one that combines generation ('I have given birth') with the overwhelming state of being both in suffering and in healing.

Her successors as poets, storytellers, philosophers, theologians and psychologists (et al.) have continued to engage the problem of grief: what it means, why it matters, how it matters, what we can do about it. Concepts of grief have shifted form and focus across the millennia, but its impact seems to have remained pretty much what it always has been: an assault on the self, the anguish of having to re-construct one's experience of the world, following a huge loss.

Some two millennia after Enheduanna broached the subject in writing, and jumping over the many many writers who pursued the same topic, we come to the sixteenth-century philosopher Michel de Montaigne who opens his essay 'On sadness' with a rather curt dismissal of those who suffer the weight of sorrow:

> I neither like it nor think well of it, even though the world, by common consent, has decided to honour it with special favour. Wisdom is decked out in it; so are Virtue and Conscience – a daft and monstrous adornment ... a quality which is ever harmful, ever mad. (1991: 58)

Really? Ever harmful, ever mad? Of course, Montaigne was not the first or the last to treat grief as a taboo topic or emotion (see, e.g., Ivy 2022; Lambrecht & Wendling 2022). And after this opening salvo, he demonstrates a genuine understanding of how sorrow works. Drawing on both history and myth, he observes the radical pain occasioned by the loss of loved ones. He cites a story recounted by Erasmus: the tale of Psammenitus, a king of Egypt who was captured by the king of Persia.[1] Reportedly, Psammenitus 'remained quiet' when watching his daughter taken into slavery and his son to execution but broke down in tears when he saw a friend in the line of captives. Montaigne explains: 'The truth is that he was already brimful of sadness, so the least extra burden broke down the barriers of his endurance' (1991: 58).

The burden of grief can do more than break one's endurance; Montaigne recounts another story, about a military officer who saw his son killed in battle, and as he tells it, 'the violent strain of that sadness froze his vital spirits and, just as he was, toppled him dead to the ground' (1991: 59). Which does indeed happen, 20th-century research shows: people do indeed die of 'broken heart' syndrome, in statistically significant numbers (Ennis & Majid 2019).

Montaigne then draws on myth, turning to the story of Niobe. She brought herself to the attention of the gods by averring that she was better than the gods because she was the mother of seven sons and seven daughters. In a violent overreaction, the gods

---

[1] This is sourced from the Apophthegmata; varie mixta: Diversum Graecorum, IX (Opera, 1703–6, Vol. IV, col. 304EF)

slaughtered all her children; her husband then killed himself in his sorrow; and she herself, overcome by grief, was turned to stone that continued to weep marble tears (Ovid 1899: 149-76). Such grief is the *ad absurdum* example of that 'sad, deaf, speechless stupor which seizes us when we are overwhelmed by tragedies beyond endurance' (Montaigne 1991: 59); which is also his key argument about why it is better not to grieve.

Subsequent research and philosophical argument largely disagree with Montaigne, though most acknowledge that grief is potentially harmful. Philosopher Martha Nussbaum, for instance, describes 'the messy material of grief and love' (2001: 1), and those two 'messy' emotions are inextricably interconnected. For Jacques Derrida, who wrote so much on death and grieving, 'Philia' (or love) 'begins with the possibility of survival ... for one does not survive without mourning' (1997: 13). We cannot enter into love without realising that survival is not on the cards; one or other of us will die, and the other mourn. As Nussbaum says, later in her work: 'the grief we feel is proportional to the extent of the loss. People grieve only mildly for a person who has been a small part of their lives' (2001: 55). If we love, we will mourn. But if mourning is the price we pay for love, it's worth it.

The 20th and early 21st centuries have been characterised by a corpus of research into grief and mourning, and a range of findings from these investigations. Sigmund Freud's famous essay, 'Mourning and melancholia' (1959), offers a starting point for many such studies, particularly those that focus on finely slicing the definitions for the various terms we use about grief. Freud's thesis distinguishes mourning from melancholia on evaluative as well as practical grounds: mourning, for Freud, is natural and necessary, something time will remedy. Melancholia (or depression), on the other hand, has a pathological quality because, he writes, for the melancholic, reality is suspended: while the mourner accepts that the loved one is lost forever, the melancholic grieves for the phantasm of a happily-ever-after (1959: 249).

Developments in health and psychology are still, to some extent, coloured by this. We see it in Elisabeth Kübler-Ross' famous (if now debunked) five stages of grief (1969), which posits a linear approach, where the end point is the Freudian 'realist principle' of acceptance. We see it too in the diagnosis of 'prolonged grief disorder', which designates appropriate grieving as being short term. Mughal, Azhar, Mahon and Siddiqui open their 2023 article on this 'disorder' with the rather cool comment that:

> Most individuals recover adequately within a year after the loss; however, some individuals experience an extension of the grieving process. This condition, identified as prolonged grief disorder, results from failure to transition from acute to integrated grief.

Grieving as failure. We need to 'get over it'; we need to 'work through it'; we need to 'move past it'. But grief is not simply a process; it is a way of being. And even the Stoics, those rejecters of the messiness of emotion, understood something important about grief. Nussbaum cites the Stoic Chrysippus as having observed that grief:

> contains not only the judgment that an important part of my life has gone, but that *it is right* to be upset about it ... It asserts the real value of the [lost] object, it says that getting upset is a response to something really important, not just a whim. (2001: 47; emphasis in original)

When we grieve, we are right to grieve. Grief is both universal and existential, a response to a very wide range of losses, experienced across many dimensions of any individual's life (Guldin & Leget 2023). And we each grieve in our own way, not least because, as Derrida observed, 'each death is unique, of course, and therefore unusual' (2001: 193).

There is little that can accelerate the most acute states of grieving – the being 'brimful of sadness', in Montaigne's words.

But there is some consolation, some palliative intervention, offered by story, poem, or art. As creatives, we can articulate our pain and our loss, however complex this action; and we should do so. As Derrida writes, 'Speaking is impossible, but so too would be silence or absence or a refusal to share one's sadness' (1989: xvi). If my grief 'is too much for me', then arguably the creative expression of it might reduce the pain to 'It is enough for me' – something with which I can live. As readers too we can be consoled by reminders, in poetry and other arts, of the universality of grief; and the deep love and connection that continues, albeit radically changed, after the loss of those we love. We can be reminded too that, much as others have accommodated themselves to this new world of grief, we too may find a way to live with it: not necessarily better, not necessarily broken, but changed.

Works Cited

Derrida, Jacques 1989 *Memoires for Paul de Man* (rev. ed.; trans C Lindsay, J Culler, E Cadava and P Kamuf), New York, NY: Columbia University Press

Derrida, Jacques 1997 *Politics of Friendship* (trans George Collins), New York, NY: Verso

Derrida, Jacques 2001 *The Work of Mourning*, ed. Pascale-Anne Brault and Michael Nass, Chicago, IL: University of Chicago Press

Ennis, Jeffrey & Umair Majid 2019 '"Death from a broken heart": A systematic review of the relationship between spousal bereavement and physical and physiological health outcomes', *Death Studies* 45.7: 538–51, https://doi.org/10.1080/07481187.2019.1661884

Freud, Sigmund 1959 'Mourning and melancholia', in *The Complete Psychological Works of Sigmund Freud, Vol XIV*, London: Hogarth Press, 237–60

Guldin, Mai-Britt & Carlo Leget 2023 'The integrated process model of loss and grief – An interprofessional understanding', *Death Studies* 48.7: 738–52, https://doi.org/10.1080/07481187.2023.2272960

Hallo, William W & JJA van Dijk 1968 *The Exaltation of Inanna*, New Haven, CT: Yale University Press

Ivy, Diana K 2022 'Grief as Taboo: Lewis, Burleson, and the Communication of Grief', in GD Luurs (ed.), *Handbook of Research on Communication Strategies for Taboo Topics*, Hershey, PA: IGI Global, 441–58

Kübler-Ross, Elisabeth 2003 [1969] *On Death and Dying: What the Dying Have to Teach Doctors, Nurses, Clergy and Their Own Families*, New York, NY: Scribner

Lambrecht, Bram & Miriam Wendling 2022 'Grief, Identity, and the Arts in the West: An Introduction', in Lambrecht & Wendling (eds), *Grief, Identity, and the Arts: A multidisciplinary Perspective on Expressions of Grief*, Leiden: Brill, 1–12

Montaigne, Michel de 1991 [1603] 'On Sadness', in *The Complete Essays* (trans MA Screech), London: Penguin

Mughal, Saba, Yusra Azhar, Margaret M Mahon, & Waqas J Siddiqui 2023 'Grief Reaction and Prolonged Grief Disorder', *StatPearls* (14 November), https://www.ncbi.nlm.nih.gov/books/NBK507832/, accessed 24 April 2025

Nussbaum, Martha 2001 *Upheavals of Thought: The Intelligence of Emotions*, Cambridge: Cambridge University Press

Ovid 1899 [c.8CE] 'Niobe and Her Children', in *The Metamorphoses* (trans HT Riley), Philadelphia, PA: Sherman & Co

Aegean Blues

PAUL HETHERINGTON

*Grief is ... like a window that will
simply open of its own accord*
— Arthur Golden —

*We used to have a nickname for the sense of
inadequacy and accidie . . . the "Aegean Blues"*
— John Fowles —

I.

The girl on the ferry looks left to the harbour as I watch you on this fractious ocean. It's as if, in affection, we approach a long-hidden idea, rising like a city within our blood – and blood's corpuscles and the corpuscles of light show whitewashed buildings. We know them as intimately as we know each other, in a landscape scattered with hewn stone. Fondness and grief embodied at once – a testing inheritance.

2.

We're ensconced in arrival – and though the first blue evening is slow to come, it's a form of witness we adore like penitents searching salvation. Even an implacable statue would be moved by this sky's blood infusion, falling and tumbling through saturations. Our emotions redden, light surrounds our bodies as a form of immersion; we spill into heartache. An hour later there's a weird airiness with the blue cast of truth.

3.

Your new distress is for your thrown-off life. Yet you'll return to its familiar lineaments and its idea of 'home' – though the prospect saddens in this shadowed evening as you ask exactly what colour it is. A hue of fraught feeling, a hint of steel, a sense of pain the ancients chiselled: 'What greater sorrow than being forced to leave behind my native earth?' The way words drop into precipitous silence.

* 'What greater sorrow. . .' is from *Electra* by Euripedes

4.

This place stands for promise, or so you say: of what you'd never imagined you'd see, even while conjuring a thousand vistas. It opposes what crawls in your DNA and suggests 'I belong' – once an uncomfortable phrase – is right for this place and its ineffable light. You say the phrase through the blue in your eyes, addressing the wash that paints the sea – fulfilment and sorrow are soon the same.

5.

Four bells hold the breeze in a tolling trance. Air drops heat like remembrance – 'I know from Australia this sense of compression; of standing in sweat while wanting a way of transporting my life.' Here, we've finally arrived at a shore, our stale hopes vanquished by examining light. Grief fringes feeling; the bells' chimes rouse and chide.

6.

Sculptures sing with intolerable sounds – laments from the old world carried to an encroaching morning; ghosts pulling language from our mouths; our griefs emerging from hibernation. The museum's plinthed choir tells us of loss we've brought together across the Aegean; a reciprocal knowledge we barely shared. It's a joyous agony to confront the emergence, like a discordant song.

7.

Even in noon's fluctuating heat there's the secret promise of evening's blue. We're enamoured, speaking of what's to come, finding connection in ethereal feeling. Yet your sadness rises at the prospect of languor, and you tell me a history jagged with regret. A hallucinatory present; past's blue delirium.

8.

We're standing in water, pulling at light, and the flicker of surfaces climbs in our eyes. You duck under water and I'm chasing your body with my camera lens. Yet we see very little as sunlight blinds and stones relay their coruscations. Our bodies sense their mortalities as the clockface turns and hours enlarge.

9.

Your private grief quietly returns. A sense of your inheritance forgetting you; a longing for elusive feeling. We share it like a bitter chocolate, dissolving it slowly, tasting it on our speaking tongues, asking ourselves what we appreciate of sorrow's cargo. Later we swim in the bumping ocean as evening posits imponderable light. You ask uncertainly, 'Resolution blue?' We kiss our agreement.

10.

The agonies won't leave, so we continue to heft them – even in happiness – like unwieldy luggage. Yet in a spa we put them aside for two or three hours – 'I'm contented here'. It doesn't sit easily and soon we dress in the old anguish again, pricked and piqued by their returning colours – blue, black and an abject grey. Night quickly follows.

11.

'I have it within me constantly.' We're eating
sardines and watching a sky like a spilled artist's
palette: 'I can't contain this sadness that rises.'
It spills from your gestures and peers through
your eyes – a sense of invasive, ghosting absence.
'The uncanny has hold, in a kind of kidnap.'
The Aegean blue wraps, like a blanket.

12.

'I'm home when away.' We climb the hill to stand in thrall at a cliff's open mouth, showing the ocean. 'Once a haven for pirates, where my absconding feelings might find respite.' I smile at the metaphor, and we enter a museum of Bronze Age remains, including dwellings: 'Will that old mirror show my likeness?'

13.

The Aegean evening flares beside us and we know our bodies won't let this go, no matter how far we travel away; and that the feelings made here won't disappear. We know we've taken into our blood what eyes have encountered – intromission as the ancients proposed it. How to leave beauty that's writhing within us?

14.

As water polishes your bobbing arms, I see a cat on the pool's raised surround next to your shoulder. Ginger and white, it stoops to press its nose to your face, but halts, unsure of the dancing water below. We're reminded of how we too would nuzzle against the bobbing refractions of evening, sensing affection reaching between us as if lying between outstretched paws.

15.

As if we lay between stretched paws, we decline to rise, even as afternoon shoves aside morning; even as yesterday's plans depart. You say you'd stay here forever, turning in the bed to reach your book. We read a nineteenth-century novel aloud and you nod, 'That's like me.' This intricate pleasure of chasing old words, refurbishing loss.

16.

Grief knows us unequally, yet we share its
discord, even while searching for renewal and
promise – feeding cats on a low stone wall,
finding groves that once sheltered gods, and
an ancient arena where plays were performed.
You're transfigured there as if in a mask, your
hair tied closely by sunset's last rags.

17.

'How do we speak of what we know?' I suggest we don't try; that we wait for words to find us again in a notional future. The light seems to see us – and even see through us – as it rolls through the sky. It's as if it's a single, encompassing eye – yet only later do we share this impression. 'Do you see me clearly?' you ask from the bed. 'Am I even visible?'

18.

Evening arrives as if an eyelid's half-closing; as if what's been glimpsed of our stone-made terrace is now barely seen. 'I'm frightened,' you say, 'of leaving here; and scared of what approaches.' We say no more, sipping wine, avoiding the intimations of peripheral vision.

19.

Waiting outside, we drink neat gin from a water bottle until the sky begins to reel. Departure waits like a broken promise. We hardly speak, nursing a sense of stalled recovery, finding griefs returning like wraiths. 'Love,' you say, 'lives like a jag in the guts. Even after a year, I pick up the phone, then remember the void at the end of the call. The words I would say cannot expand.' The taxi arrives and we gather our bags.

20.

>We would speak of affection but sit in silence. The taxi turns and we watch the Aegean. I imagine triremes rowing away. This ravaged world; the beauty it holds in museums and hillsides, climbs into mind, as if the past underlines its yield.

21.

Leaving you is to take loss by the hand, as a ferry's wash collars my dreams. Your fingers remain imprinted on my arm. At the airport our farewells fall through decades. I glance at the departure board, not taking it in.

Complicated

OZ HARDWICK

*I used to be of humankind
I had a life to lead,
But now I'm frozen in a dream,
My life is lost, it seems.*
– Robert Calvert (Hawkwind) –

CONTENTS

An Inventory of Small Denials 29

One Night in Soho 30

Sorry You Were Out 31

The Little Things 32

Out of Sight 33

The Alarm Clock Ticks 34

Smashed 35

Traces 36

Assessing the Damage 37

The Functionality of Teenage Poetry 38

Bargain 39

My Own Good Samaritan 40

Partial Illumination 41

The End of Innocence 42

The Dead Wood Stage 43

A Matter of Genre 44

The Third Stroke 45

True Story 46

What Doesn't Kill You 47

The Routemaster Epiphany 48

Endnote 49

An Inventory of Small Denials

The roll call is complicated by the lack of the living, but I've come to a workable arrangement of dried flowers and strips torn from fashions of the past. Twigs bound in ribbons on railings, all day, every day, line up in row upon row, smiling sadly like the fat full moon. Pressed petals, stiff as old car doors, answer in yellow when I invite them to speak. *We blew in smoke rings across Salisbury Plain, our heads light with music. Remember the closeness, and the ache humming like a struck wineglass. Remember waking alone in the blazing solstice sun.* My skin blooms carnation as I articulate names of the dead. *Here. Here. Here.*

One Night in Soho

Above the umbrella, the stars. Here we are, my arm loose around your shoulder, gliding through London, for all the world like lovers. Naturally, there's music, warm and rising like birds at sunrise, breaking the cage of my breast: and, of course, even the rain is singing as it stirs smiling passers-by, urging them to the edge of dance. And, inevitably, I can't see the stars through the umbrella and the rain: and, besides, I'm watching all those strangers as they synchronise their steps and begin to spin, and I'm glancing at the way your hair sways as we sashay those final few steps to the station. Freeze. A monochrome snap. The final note holds for forty years until, at last, the stars break through, and I wish you were here to see them.

Sorry You Were Out

Grief, when it arrives, is an engine idling in the street: a taxi or a police car; or maybe just a white van with its windows wound down, its radio playing a song the whole world's forgotten. There's a knock on the door, respectful but insistent, a steady 40 bpm, without any of the flourishes a friend might add to set the mood for the afternoon. When I was a child, I loved clocks, and had seven in my tiny box room, from a folding travel alarm with a faux leather case, to a cuckoo clock crowned with an antlered stag. No one else could stand it, but when I couldn't sleep, I found comfort in the cross-rhythms and accents, the shifting stresses and implied melodies. I grew to understand the ticking like language, translating the night and all its knowledge of time; so, when the steady beat repeats on the door, I don't need to answer. I know that the taxi driver has turned on his light and is checking his mirrors, that the police officer has closed his eyes on his every small regret, and that even the DJ has already forgotten that song. The street is quiet, but I know that when I finally open the door there will be a box wrapped in brown paper, tied with simple string. It will be neither heavy nor light, and when I hold it to my ear, it will tick like a cooling engine or a schoolboy's first wristwatch.

The Little Things

In the pub by the sea, the music plays a touch too fast. No one else appears to notice, as they tuck into Sunday lunch. It's not Sunday, but they don't notice that, either, and they don't notice the windswept couple who have just blown in from forty years in the future, giggling like kids at the singer who sounds like a drunken mouse. Forty years. It sounds like a lot, or like nothing at all: the lapse between now and the Miners' Strike, or then and the Second World War. During the War, frightened families gathered here, weeping for the devastation across the narrow estuary. During the Strike, we caught a train to the sea and the insuperable heights of loftiest shade, a neat facsimile of Paradise, where the music played a touch too fast. What a time it was, and here we are again, laughing as if this could last forever, laughing like you might not be carried away by a moonlight shadow.

Out of Sight

Grief's at the window now, beast-eyed and wheedling to come in. I hear it in the night, its low animal howl ruffling the curtains and setting my teeth on edge, keeping me awake, or maybe keeping me asleep; and I smell it in the day, its metallic musk catching in my throat and putting me off eating. Though I keep it locked outside, I somehow find shed claws hooked in the furniture, and I have to scoop its scabby hairs from all the plugholes for fear of flooding the whole unbearable world. I tried laying traps, but they filled with flailing sparrows. Then, I laid out poison, but the garden died. So, I bought a gun from a man in the pub, but it's grief's finger on the trigger and the barrel's so cold against the roof of my mouth.

The Alarm Clock Ticks

The last hour of the night stretches to snapping point, then holds. I feel it like it's my own skin, and I will it to just *go on and fucking break*, because at least pain has firm hands and shows its face in the mirror. But it still holds, and outside this incredible shrinking room all the cars and birds are sleeping from here to the end of the world, and all the dead are pretending to be alive. In the middle of some waste ground, earmarked for development then cast away, a ghost writes ice with a white finger on the glass of an incongruous call box: and when my phone doesn't ring, I answer it and, as always, she says nothing. If I was a rock star in a sleazy LA hotel, this is the moment I'd launch the TV through the panoramic window. Instead, I hurl myself into tumultuous stillness and brace myself for the eruption of glass.

Smashed

When I smashed smashed the glass, it was not what I what I expected, echoes reverberating echoes echoes down the corridor deep inside, in me, I thought, as if as if as if light was taking shape and falling falling, though it would make no sense if I said spoke the words words words aloud loud. I looked and saw my knuckles bleeding smashed like glass falling echoing falling red to the floor.

Traces

This, then, is what remains: a book, a birthday badge, and a few photographs separated by twenty years. Here you are, striding through the world, walking on water, walking on air, walking into a future to be built from books like stepping stones, one story at a time. And here you are again, blowing out candles, and pinning experience onto your winter lapel. There's music round the edges of every picture, but I can't hear the words after all this time. The book is marked in pencil, but I can't recall the significance of the phrases underlined. I feel, as always, everything and nothing, again and again, walking into the past, while I press the steel pin hard into my palm.

Assessing the Damage

The consultant rises from the depth of the well, her rheumy orbs swimming with a million years of knowledge that no one should have to bear. She asks me about my grief and my silence, their weight in my chest, and the degree to which they swallow light. I can't speak – I could never speak – so she gives me a pen and a thorn to prick my wrist. There is no paper to be found, so I write on the air that sags between us: *When the Sun came, I melted. When the rain came, I dissolved. When the wind blew like a soldier's breath on the last morning of peace, I froze. But all the time I felt something – which was nothing – growing inside, like grass seed in an eggshell or cress on blotting paper, green and barely substantial.* She sighs like a sign at a ghost town hotel, her veined eyes glowing like lamps in a storm. We both know the symptoms, the root cause, the proliferation of cliché, and the impossibility of effecting a cure. I try to speak but can't. *Well*, she says, and draws me into the dark water.

The Functionality of Teenage Poetry

Later, the living room's cold as deep space, so there's nothing left to do but burn the poems. I'm not talking daffodils and ancient mariners, which we all know without actually reading them, and I don't mean those accusatory rhymes with emphatic rhythmic gestures to bang home their blatant accusations. And I certainly don't mean those experimental chapbooks swapped at readings in empty coffee shops, with nodding heads and clicking fingers. What I'm talking about here are the poems written on basement walls and scratched into phone box windows, the poems written on green paper towels from factory washrooms, and the poems written in hotel biros on the inside of raw wrists. No one remembers a single line, and the flesh and blood of their unnamed subject is just a handful of photos and a few kilobytes of saved emails, but if I could just strike two words together to catch a spark, their fire could thaw the ice that keeps me sealed here like a lost astronaut.

Bargain

Determined to declutter, I set out my stall to sell my imperfect memories. Here's a silver ring with a small blue stone, slipped from finger to finger in the shadow of monumental folly. Here's a book of pithy quotations by famous people with nothing to say. Here's a bedside lamp made from a human head, its glowing eyes kind and its lips still whispering blessings. Here's the entire eighteenth century, still sealed in its original packaging. I said these memories were imperfect, but see how they shine in the market lanterns, feel how reassuring they are to the touch. No cash or card, each one is going for a song, and the fiddler is tuning her solemn violin.

My Own Good Samaritan

Each morning, my reflection in shop windows recedes a little further, my face tilting away from the light as it studiously avoids my eyes. My analyst tells me to make friends with the slow loss, and that such occurrences are perfectly normal. I'm at that age at which every day brims with epiphanies and grand revelations, but each time she says *normal*, I weep like a pilgrim who has crawled for miles on hands and knees to kiss the ragged hem of the sacred. This, she tells me, resting her index finger lightly on my forehead, is also normal. And so, in the evening, when those same windows fill with nothing but sunset, blazing like consecrated wine, the only reflection I see is my analyst, stamping out a cigarette with her bare feet as she opens her car door. It is dark for this time of year. It is always dark. It is always this time of year. There is someone in the passenger seat who appears to be laughing or crying, though it's hard to tell which, as they're wearing a mask that's crudely cut from the face I used to wear when I could still look myself in the eye.

Partial Illumination

A Zippo flicks in a lonely room, each spark illuminating a different detail. Sheets rumpled back on themselves. An unread book. A scattering of bright pins. A teacup stained into a limnological chart of the Styx. The flame doesn't catch, but each snatched glimpse is a Kim's game of consequences, a flash of a collage collapsing into chaos. Whose room is this, that holds such absence? Whose thumb is this, blistering on the stiff wheel? A fine flower folded from purple paper. A purple taper that has never been lit. A mirror reflecting a mirror, with a flicker of a face, too fleeting to read. A numb thumb, forever wheeling. Don't ask whose room this is. Don't pretend you don't already know.

The End of Innocence

My head is a house built from smoke and loss, brick by grey brick, its windows glazed with mist. It stands on a street carved through clouds and fog, or through dirty rain smeared on smudged bus windows, as imagined empires teeter to war. Gables pitch to ash and secrets, and the charcoal chimney's a finger pressed to pursed lips. Overhead, the sky's awash with warning birds, singing songs of scissors, slicing their nests from pulped newsprint and fairy tales unfit for fretful children. Strangers in striped pyjamas call, rapping at doors they bring themselves, rattling reports of echoing silence. They enter, uninvited, but find themselves still outside. Meanwhile, I shuffle, a mute insomniac, from room to identical room. Even the ghosts have gone, leaving only their eyes.

The Dead Wood Stage

The fourth stage of grief is the dead wood stage, with the ghost of Doris Day chivvying me into unwilling action with a whip and a 500-watt smile. I tell her I don't want to eat, and that I can't face calling to whoever that is far off in the bathroom mirror. *Que sera, sera*, she says, and tells me with a wink how her dancing career shattered like young bone when a train hit her car. I explain that I feel like dead wood: the log that even the cartoon bugs shun, or the stick that Pooh would drop from the bridge and would never be seen again. She laughs and tells me I'm just losing focus, but my throat's as dry as a desert thistle in May and, besides, this is a woman who once dated Ronald Reagan and last appeared in a Wham! hit video forty years ago. Her eyes shine as she reminds me that, once upon a time, we were both young, we both had secret loves, and we both shone in glorious Technicolor. *I could paint the leaves*, I say, *but the wood will still be dead.*

A Matter of Genre

I seal the gaps in my days with simple tasks, like balling socks and washing dishes, but still the dark seeps in. It pushes the air from the room, and then from my body, then presses on my shoulders like a cruel lover until I fold and flatten. It's the same every day, and if I was a ditzy rom-com blonde, this is when we'd cut to a bright café with girlfriends and bagels and wise and witty banter. But the colour's bled out, and I'm just a single cell from a pre-code shocker: a sordid room with an unmade bed, a smoking gun, and a broken window where the dark floods in.

The Third Stroke

In search of the once-familiar, I am relearning telephone boxes and their precise occurrences in the predominantly urban landscape. It's not about the queues or the sour smell that everyone recalls, nor even the broken glass, but the simple red weight where one street meets another, and even the most passionate adherent of Robert Frost wouldn't be able to say which road was less travelled by. When I was a child, my head awash with distant voices and my knees scored with playgrounds, I was stabbed near the heart with a 2H pencil and, this being before the days of hospitals or even faith healing, I hied me to a phone box for seven times seven summers, each longer than its predecessor. Of course, I fell in love with the voice of the speaking clock, and I'd place my hands at ten-to-two on her plastic shoulders as we danced to a new song every day. How could I have forgotten all those years? But it's never too late to be late, and I'm slowly relearning all this iron certainty. I ask not for whom the bell rings. After all this time, it's once again for me.

True Story

After our mutual acquaintance's party, I lie on the floor and feel nothing. I feel its shape and its soft weight at my shoulder, breathing smoke. I feel its slight biography moving through the streets of architects' plans of the city of the future, with underground trains that sigh like opening curtains and neon billboards advertising dream homes for all. I feel its voice warming the air around vibrating phone boxes, closing the cracks between paving slabs, and smoothing the contours between Friday nights and the dawn of the Aquarian Age. It's – what? – maybe twenty-five years since the party and, when the postman passes like a priest on the other side of the imagined street, I feel nothing take my hand, as if I was a butterfly trapped in a nightclub, and lift me softly towards a sunlit window.

What Doesn't Kill You

Relief arrives at unexpected moments. Emails storm the streets like the Pamplona bulls, fearful and angry, red-eyed, and with red exclamation marks branded between their horns, yet I feel the paradoxical bliss of feeling nothing at all. Or, the train is delayed, then cancelled, and then men in overalls arrive to rip up the track and redevelop the station for compact urban living. One of the men steals my phone, and a storm boils over like a vision of Hell. I shake the last cigarette from a pack I bought from a pub vending machine in the last century, hold it to the sky to catch the passing lightning, then sit on a newly-painted bench to take stock of the unlikely calm. What doesn't kill you may possibly make you stronger, though it's more likely to present a mild temporary inconvenience, or even unanticipated benefits. More likely still, it may pass by completely unnoticed. One of those emails is from someone I loved and lost, and I momentarily consider turning up on her doorstep with a bunch of flowers and a storm behind my eyes. But there are buildings, buildings, buildings between here and that other world, and no one even remembers that in the old days there were trains. I expel the stale smoke from my lungs. It's a relief.

The Routemaster Epiphany

I never trusted buses: the enforced proximity to strangers, and the inherent uncertainty born of filthy windows. Once, as a child, I was so befuddled on my way to the orthodontist that I couldn't alight for days, and every time anyone leaned into my personal space to offer assistance, I shrank back further into the seat, until eventually no one noticed me anymore. I'd still be there now, but the bus was decommissioned and sold off to a bunch of hippies, who set me free at the nearest railway station with a pouch of hallucinogenic mushrooms and my train fare home. My family welcomed me like a scene from the Bible, though with a vegan option for fatted calf, and I never caught a bus again. Until, that is, you died, and your face appeared on the side of the Number 9, clear as a broken Brexit promise. Trusting to this vision, I paid my pensioner fare and climbed the stairs to where schoolkids were still scrapping and the men and women off the early shift were still smoking as they pored over daily papers. I sat at the front, the best seat in the house, and you sat down beside me. One of those hippies from way, way back – about 80 now, but wiry and tough, with mischievous eyes as sharp as a crow – passed us a roll-up and smiled. Outside, streetlights glowed, but I couldn't see where we were going. For the first time, it didn't matter.

Endnote

Trusting to this vision, relief arrives at unexpected moments. I feel nothing take my hand, my head awash with distant voices and wise and witty banter. I explain that I feel like dead wood, built from smoke and loss, a teacup stained into a limnological chart of the Styx. I'm at that age at which every day brims with pithy quotations by famous people with nothing to say. What I'm talking about here are the poems written on basement walls, swimming with a million years of knowledge that no one should have to bear. I feel, as always, everything and nothing, as if light was taking shape and falling from here to the end of the world, its low animal howl ticking like language, translating the night and all its knowledge of time. Your hair sways as we sashay those final few steps to the station. The roll call is complicated by a lack of the living.

(O)bituary:
The Little Deaths

CASSANDRA ATHERTON

*I never intended to have an orgasm.
Believe me – it just showed up.*
— Nin Andrews —

*I will live in thy heart, die in thy lap,
and be buried in thy eyes.*
— William Shakespeare —

CONTENTS

1. Wine Cellar 55
2. Aeroplane 56
3. Trampoline 57
4. Candy Shop 58
5. Fiat 59
6. Ferris Wheel 60
7. Kitchen Bench 61
8. Lido 62
9. Dressing Room 63
10. Planetarium 64
11. Tree House 65
12. Shower 66
13. Cemetery 67
14. Breakfast Buffet 68
15. Gym 69
16. Library 70
17. Merry-go-round 71
18. Park 72
19. Elevator 73
20. Laundromat 74
21. Golf Course 75

1.

ATHERTON, Cassandra – *la petite mort, 3rd March, 2019, in the wine cellar.* As he slept, she snuck into his wine cellar, popping the lock with a bobby pin and wiggling the latch free. Huddling into its cool gloom, the cement floor imprinted a grid on the balls of her bare feet. Wine racks were wooden catacombs; a temporary holding space. He once told her a lower hydrogen level meant a greater potential for ageing, so they made love beneath an oak tree. In the wine cellar she traced the borders of an empty box before climbing inside its darkness. She felt its shape settle around her, waiting for him to roll her smooth tannins on his tongue.

2.

ATHERTON, Cassandra – *la petite mort, 23rd September, 2023, on an aeroplane.* He went down on her in the back row of a Qantas flight to Dallas. Once the seatbelt sign was extinguished, he pushed back their shared arm rest while she adjusted her blanket as if pulling in darkness. People on either side were watching movies or dozing as she wiggled her pants lower, the blanket's constraint like a tightening cocoon. She closed her eyes as his breath fogged the inside of her thighs.

3.

ATHERTON, Cassandra – *la petite mort, 11th December, 1997, on the trampoline.* In the first week of the summer holidays, she scaled the fence of the outdoor trampoline park and let him in through the gate. Pulling off their shorts, they sat on the blue trampoline mat with their limbs around each other, bouncing and lifting. As they built momentum, their locked bodies were as high as the fence she'd climbed. When their twinned buttocks rebounded from the mat, she flipped him onto his back, with subsiding reverberations.

4.

ATHERTON, Cassandra – *la petite mort, 3rd July, 2016, in Captain Jonny's Candy Shop.* There was no one on the upper floor when she followed the barrels of technicolour candy up the stairs. He held the bag open as she scooped samples, letting them slide across his hands. She heard the loose sugar shiver in the bottom of the bag. She kissed him between the giant gummy bears and sour rainbow straps, taking the paper bag from his hands and balancing it on a nearby barrel of fried egg gummies. In a glucose haze she pulled up her dress, and his kisses were sticky on her stomach. As he moved lower, he reached up to place a marshmallow candy in her mouth, muffling her cries.

5.

ATHERTON, Cassandra – *la petite mort, 3rd June, 2013, in a red Fiat 500.* After his fingers burrowed through the tiny Os of her fishnet stockings, she rolled them down her hips. He parked under a Jacaranda tree and placed the windshield protector across the glass – a reflective silver concertina. She climbed between seats, from front passenger side to the back. He unwound a window so his feet wouldn't push against the glass as her toes grazed the roof. In the afternoon light, her body was a suffused, electric pink.

6.

ATHERTON, Cassandra – *la petite mort, 7th September, 1995, on the ferris wheel.* He popped a button on her long olive coat as he pressed his knee between her legs. She heard the clink on the bottom of the carriage as the disc spun off the edge. They were a third of the way to the top, the shadows of spokes and struts snagging on their bodies. With her coat pulled up to her waist and stockings binding her ankles, she free-fell into his arms, the ferris wheel's car stuttering and swinging. Turning her head, she watched the rollercoaster chasing its circular track before she catapulted into the dark, lit sky.

7.

ATHERTON, Cassandra – *la petite mort, 23rd September, 2000, against the kitchen bench.* Drinking champagne, she placed her hands on either side of the glass as he lifted up the back of her dress. With a hand around her waist, he pushed her feet apart with his own and leaned into her. As she shuddered, champagne bubbled from her nose, spotting the marble bench and dripping onto his naked toes.

8.

ATHERTON, Cassandra – *la petite mort, 31st March, 1996, at the Lido.* They waded into the horizon until they felt no separation from its incandescence. Floating on their backs, they were nearly parallel lines joining sea and sky. Then, in the lapping of water, their limbs distorted in a frilling of fingers and toes. He encouraged her legs around his waist like an ouroboros and, in that moment they were a blurring of desire, their bodies slippery and warm. He lowered his hands and her cries rose like birds returning home.

9.

ATHERTON, Cassandra – *la petite mort, 18th November, 1991, in the dressing room.* She was Ophelia in her high school play, reviewed as better mad than maid. Backstage, on closing night, she invited Polonius to her dressing room. He brought the arras with him for privacy. Behind it, he pulled flowers from her hair while she undid his breeches. When he reached past the split in her dress, her head fell back and she moaned, 'Hey nonny nonny'.

10.

ATHERTON, Cassandra – *la petite mort, 20th November, 2016, in the Konika Minolta Planetarium.* She drank a Venus cocktail in the lobby and ate a bag of Milky Way Cotton Candy. When she poked out her tongue, he said it fizzed with flavour like a fruit tingle. Inside the circular auditorium a string quartet played the slow movement of Beethoven's 21st piano concerto while pink and purple clouds lurched on the ceiling and walls. In the darkness, his fingers played a concerto on her thigh and edged her voluminous skirt.

11.

ATHERTON, Cassandra – *la petite mort, 10th July, 2000, in the tree house.* Her limbs stuck out through the windows of the tiny wooden structure, while his head nudged the ceiling. There was a pack of playing cards under one of her buttocks and the remnants of a McHappy meal under the other. When he touched her, she resembled Alice 'opening out like the largest telescope'. He knocked over the plastic tea set and green cordial stained her dress; she told him to continue. Her toes twitched and the tree dropped all its red leaves.

12.

ATHERTON, Cassandra – *la petite mort, 28th May, 2016, in the shower.* The tiles were cold against her back and his skin was hot. She spat out water and breathed in steam, exhaling long, gurgling vowels like sudden grief.

13.

ATHERTON, Cassandra – *la petite mort, 27th February, 1994, in a cemetery.* In her Goth phase, she dyed her hair black and rubbed etchings from the headstones in her local necropolis. She preferred those written in gold on smooth black marble – they absorbed heat and reminded her of Poe's 'The Raven'. She took her boyfriend to Walter Lindrum's billiards table memorial and measured her naked spine against the marble cue. With one foot in each of the table's marble pockets he took time to line up before making the shot. A long shiver fluttered across her shoulder blades and exited her curled toes.

14.

ATHERTON, Cassandra – *la petite mort, 30th September, 2018, at the breakfast buffet.* He ordered soft poached eggs on rye, and she piled a bowl with wedges of watermelon and yoghurt. He frowned when she dipped the tip of her watermelon into his egg yolk, tracing a cold teaspoon on the inside of her thigh. The hard rectangle of butter on his toast slowly became a puddle; eggy watermelon juice ran down her chin.

15.

ATHERTON, Cassandra – *la petite mort, 17th October, 2025, at the gym.* She was sweaty from the treadmill when he asked her to sit on his back while he did push ups. She tucked her legs around his chest, undulating with him as he extended his spine. After the tenth repetition, he rolled her onto the mat, placing her right leg on his left shoulder. In a deep split, her muscles tightened and released.

16.

ATHERTON, Cassandra – *la petite mort, 21st February, 1993, in the library.* Nineteenth-century classics turned her on. She liked to have sex staring at their stately spines lining the bookshelves. She was Lucy Westenra, Catherine Linton, Maggie Tulliver, Dorothea Brooke and, once a month, Emma Bovary. She called the boys Charles Bingley, St John Rivers, Philip Pirrip and even Raskolnikov. When Oliver Twist whispered *deus ex machina* into her ear, she finished quickly and left him wanting more.

17.

ATHERTON, Cassandra – *la petite mort, 6th June, 1999, on the merry-go-round.* She mounted his horse, and then him, positioning herself as a reverse cowboy. They moved up and down with the calliope music, building angular momentum. Her squeals mimicked the rollercoaster's vertiginous drop and loop.

18.

ATHERTON, Cassandra – *la petite mort, 12th December, 1999, in the park.* He unfolded a blue tarpaulin and they sat together, looking up through the branches of cherry blossom trees. They waited for the first buds to burst into flower – imagining corn kernels exploding into popcorn. He popped a bottle of champagne and they sipped it from collapsible cups. The tarpaulin crackled as she pulled him under her, popping the button of his jeans. Soft pink petals clung to her back like confetti.

19.

ATHERTON, Cassandra – *la petite mort, 27th September, 1999, in the elevator.* Muzak was her favourite music, especially classics set to pan pipes or the xylophone. He got into the lift on the sixth floor to the opening strains of *Desperado*. By the time they'd reached the twenty-fourth, they'd fogged up the mirrored walls and were singing in two-part harmony, 'you've got to let somebody love you'.

20.

ATHERTON, Cassandra – *la petite mort, 29th April, 2009, in the laundromat.* She liked the smell of fabric softener. She wanted all her lovers to smell 'classic with hints of floral and musk'. Hot, thick air clung to her skin as she jiggled coins in her palm, anxiously waiting for the washing machine's agitations to cease. She phoned him when socks were chasing t-shirts and skirts in the tumble dryer and soon he was pressing her eagerly against the machine. When her buttocks stopped tingling she put on warm underwear, before airing and folding the clothes.

21.

ATHERTON, Cassandra – *la petite mort, 1st September, 2020, on the eighteenth hole of the golf course.* She undressed next to the red flag on the seventeenth hole and waited to see if he would use his 1-iron. She liked its length and flatter trajectory. He got out of the golf buggy for a closer look at the final fairway, visualising the shot. The Bentgrass was soft as moss on her torso; his swing was smooth and powerful; she shivered like a flag in the breeze.

Modes of Mourning

JEN WEBB

They give birth astride a grave, the light gleams an instant, then it's night once more.
— Samuel Beckett —

Everywhere the dead are leaving a sign. We feel the shadow but cannot see what casts the shadow.
— Anne Michaels —

Give sorrow words: the grief that does not speak whispers the o'er-fraught heart and bids it break.
— William Shakespeare —

CONTENTS

The mourner as a child I 81
The mourner as a child II 82
The mourner as a child III 83
The mourner as a child IV 84
On funerals I 85
On funerals II 86
On funerals III 87
On funerals IV 88
Preparing the terrain I 89
Preparing the terrain II 90
Preparing the terrain III 91
Preparing the terrain IV 92
'Oh, my dead dears!' I 93
'Oh, my dead dears!' II 94
'Oh, my dead dears!' III 95
Against mourning I 96
Against mourning II 97
Against mourning III 98
Against mourning IV 99
At the end I 100
At the end II 101

The mourner as a child
I

Ignore the doctor's claim; you know that children know the work of mourning. We buried the dead wherever they appeared: those small birds, all the mice, the desiccated frogs. Mother found a shoe-box for your ragdoll, and you buried her in lieu of the new baby. She gave me silk scarves to wrap around Smoky the cat, and we buried him with tears, a bowl of kibble at his side. There was that dead snake you found on the road, and buried alongside the others in the garden. There was the teddy bear, arms gone, ear gone, fur gone: another shoe-box ceremony. We were practising. Rehearsing for the years to come.

The mourner as a child
II *(for RW)*

Winter holidays by the sea. A cottage in among dense seabush. At night the wild dogs called and cold spring tides roared, and the Kowie River knocked importunately at the door. Daytime we spilt out of the cottage to annex the dunes, test ourselves against rock walls, hurl sticks into the turbulent swirl where river meets the sea. He'd stroll outside, beer in hand, to check the tides, then set out with rods and creels for the right place on the riverbank. I brought him buckets of worms I'd dug up from the beach and looked away when he drove the hook through their bodies.

The mourner as a child
III *(for RW)*

I carried the creel, you the rod and stool, and we walked along the finger of rocks to the edge where waves rushed our feet, then retreated, then rushed again. You caught nothing but the pleasure of casting and waiting and the scent of the sea. You reached for your heart, then for the pills in your pocket, you stroked my hair saying everything is all right, and we made our way slowly up the beach, back to the house. I carried the creel. You carried your heart.

The mourner as a child
IV *(for AW)*

She woke us early, hounded us to the front room where she tuned us to mute. Behind the door, doctors hurrying to and fro; nurses setting out spells; mother turning to stone.

He was maybe dying, maybe not. I spent the six weeks of his not-dying collecting herbs and banes, communing with goldfish in the pond, asking local dogs for ideas. I wrote letters and burned them, sending the scent of their smoke to somewhere I could not describe.

Slowly he recovered. The sword hung over his head for seven more years – a mythical period – and then it fell.

On funerals
I *(for JL-C)*

After she died we planted pansies and forget-me-nots and snowdrops around her grave, selected from the list of ideal flowers that the cemetery provided. They grew and flowered and set their seed and died. Next spring they grew, and flowered, and set their seed and died. Year after year, new seedlings crowded out the ground, growing thinner and more pale until they stopped setting seed, and grass swarmed in and covered the grave.

On funerals
II *(for AB)*

We have gathered up the past you left behind. Jars of salvaged nails. Postcards mailed to your mother. A curl of your baby hair she passed to me in a ceremony of affection when our first child was born. There were photos and the manuscripts you'd prepared and the clothes we washed and folded and gave away. Your work boots and bike boots and bible and the memories we could not endure. We gathered up all we could bear to touch and sealed it in a lead-lined box and the rest we burned, agreeing never to think of it again.

On funerals
III *(for TS)*

Because the Furies watched you even in your sleep. Because the beast may have retreated but he's still waiting for the big reveal. Because when you were speaking your last words I said nothing, for fear that you'd return. God is not on your side. *We all die alone, after all*, you say, but that hardly consoles. Yesterday I called by your grave. Someone else has been visiting you: there are flowers in your vase, and fresh oranges by your headstone.

On funerals
IV

He hadn't thought to bring an umbrella; or had forgotten it, or left it somewhere, which could be anywhere for all he knows, and it's raining now, or 'pouring', says the man huddled beside him under the same tree, a man he thinks he ought to know but his eyes are too wet – too wet to be explained by the rain – and the man takes his hand, kisses it gently, promises he will be all right.

Preparing the terrain
I

A point-to-point race from dread to disaster, driving through strange country where hills are racked along the horizon like blades in a blacksmith's store, where rocks fall like pianos from the sky and the air hovers between mist and storm. In a rough field a horse, rugged up against the rain, lifts its head to watch the car pass by, its engine sluggish under your hands. You drive on, through devil's-elbow bends, in the slipstream of memories, half alert for traffic and pitfalls, sight-reading the threnody being written by crows against the clouds.

Preparing the terrain
II *(for SC)*

Three sheep tear at the grass that runs up to the dam and a peacock watches them, thoughtfully. In the next field a peahen organises her chicks, who are half grown, their adolescent tails edging toward elegance. Stop the car; your vision is letting you down. Stop the car; stand with your hand on the macrocarpa's trunk and let it convince you of calm. Don't ask: *Is it irrevocable?* The trees will answer: *It is.*

Preparing the terrain
III *(for SC)*

She has fallen again and is not doing as well as hoped. *This is to be expected*, says the nurse practitioner. We Google 'nurse practitioner'. Ah. We Google 'not doing as well as expected'. Oh. She is tottering toward infinity. *This is to be expected.* And yet it seems sudden, like when – although I know you're here in the house – your sudden cough makes me cry out and drop the coffee pot. We go back into the ward, take her hand, and say good words, bravely.

Preparing the terrain
IV

You write to tell me you are getting better. Handmade postcards, with sketches of the cabbage you have pickled for later, the seaweed you are steeping to make tea. You're back at the gym, you write, alongside a sketch of a brokeback body hoisting weights. Everything's coming up roses. You write to tell me you are moving house, changing schools. That you've joined the Party, are pulling your weight. I phone to check in on you and no one answers. I knock on your door and listen forensically to silence.

'Oh my dead dears!'[1]
I *(for JR-H)*

She was standing on the edge, looking down, which as we all shouted at her is not safe to do but she'd always prided herself on her perfect balance. She stood, then pirouetted off and floated to the beach like thistledown. Doctors lined the cliff, their faces masked with knowledge – the look we never want to see. She waved at them, then dolphined into the water and it's so long sweetheart. We believe she is living in delight, beneath the eye of the sea. Sometimes we talk about joining her but no one's game to take the first step off the cliff.

---

[1] This is Captain Cat's line, from Dylan Thomas, *Under Milkwood*

'Oh my dead dears!'
II *(for RG)*

The lightbulb in your office has guttered out. Half your books are boxed, half are shelved or scattered or face down on the desk. Your scribbled notes, tucked into books, pinned to the pinboard, stuck onto shelves. Your bus pass, coffee cup; spilt leaves from your matcha blend, their scent diffused through carpet and air. It takes a day to pack your possessions; a day to replace the bulb, to vacuum and dust and wash away all that remained. Your nameplate still on the door. Your mail still in the box.

'Oh my dead dears!'
III *(for RV)*

Those intimate dinners we held each Friday during the year all our marriages collapsed as though an earthquake had shuddered through and brought them all down. We told secret details of body incompetently addressing body, of dull anxiety, of what goes wrong. We drank too much, drank to incompetence, and then Marie could speak only French and Ron translated but only to Dutch, and I played backstop, translating into English, and our monolingual friends – Annie before she drove her car off the bridge, and Susan before she married my ex, and Chris who watched us all so closely – returned the serve, shunting back through English to Dutch to French, and repeat. Once I danced on the table, floating my skirts above my silk knickers, and Dominic stamped and sang. Once Paul lit the brandy and drank it flames and all, and then the medics arrived. Of course we were steering toward the end; and the end, when it came, was painless and sweet and then no more than shadows on the wall.

Against mourning
I *(for CB)*

Babies wrapped in satin, babies warmed by snakes, the willow crib, wicker coffin; the way baby stares too knowingly at my lens. Babies who know too much fear, and too little; babies who drink too much, cry too little.

When you choked, baby, I Heimliched you and knew I'd stopped your death, which can be stopped, I know now.

I stand in the traffic, hand erect and cry out *Stop*, and every vehicle squeals to a halt. I confront the crocodile, the shark. I examine the cancer scan, the biopsy. Burn the obit that is waiting in the wings.

Against mourning
II *(for LW)*

She is sweeping up the beach. Each early morning as sand dwellers slowly come to wakefulness she walks the edge of the sea, brushing foam back into the waves, tidying up the edges, no dust allowed below the rug, no cats secreting corpses. Like Canute she works without hope of winning. She is coming to know the voice of the sea, the voice of the sky. She is coming to know how to speak to sea creatures. She is finding the gap between self and all the sea demands.

Against mourning
III

He turns his cup around and around, gazing at maps drawn by the dregs. This feeling of sorrow, he says.

Someone responds: Sorrow: it's a finger pushing a glass toward the table's edge.

Someone else chimes in: It's a cat crying at the back door; or jolting awake from sleep. It's a solitary magpie carolling as the sun slides out of sight.

And you say: Sorrow is memories and regrets. It's the dresser drawer packed with all the everything you were never able to accomplish, it's the buses that arrive but don't stop, the buses that stop, but no one gets on or off.

Enough, he says. Too much.

Against mourning
IV *(for JSW)*

Doing the rounds of the garage sales, following the barker who stands at each intersection in the form of a corrugated card torn from a grocery box, promising pleasure if we will only stop at 12 Buriga Crescent, or 39 Maribyrnong, or unit 25 of number 51 in that new development at the back of Lawson. The pandemic is history now; no one wears a mask. We stop in Spence, on a back road that leads to the highway. It is not so much a garage sale, you suggest, as the wrapping up of a deceased estate. The son spots in you a fellow traveller, and talks you through the tables and shelves and boxes of his father's life. You buy a book, another book. You buy a shell casing someone has beaten into a vase. You buy a single medal. As we leave the man says *Wait, you'll need this*, and presses a ring into your hand, refusing cash. Back home, armed with your loupe and lights, you study it for a while, saying nothing. I think you might be weeping.

At the end

I

In a holding pattern in a whitebox room where machines are the things most alive. You are breathing though your ribs barely shift from their sleepy embrace. Heart beating, gut sifting through the slurry for food. You are in a holding pattern where LED lines on a screen tell the whole tale. Words pattern in your head but your mouth is strictly sealed. That's how it goes. Someone's hand is on your wrist. Someone's hand is on your head. Someone is making marks on a form.

At the end
II

Light wriggles past unimagined cloud, insisting on its primacy. You sit under a golf umbrella, pants drenched to darkness from hem to knee and a little water weeping on your cheeks. You don't have long to go but, you insist, you've done enough, fulfilled every expectation, satisfied almost all desires. You are ready, you insist, letting go of life as easily as a smile.

Poems of 2024-25

PAUL MUNDEN

*for Clare
and our daughter Lara*

*She may be the love that cannot hope to last
May come to me from shadows of the past*
— Herbert Kretzmer —

I / saw morning harden against the wall
— Thomas Hardy —

*Horas Avolantes Numero, Mortuos Plango;
Vivos ad Preces Voco*
— inscription on the great tenor bell,
Winchester Cathedral —

CONTENTS

Please No	107
Our Separate Ways	108
The Steps	109
Snow	110
The Submerged Cathedral	111
Black Dog	112
Blue Christmas	113
'Somewhere Only We Know'	114
Your Laugh	115
Renovation	116
Autumn Collection	117
Saint Juliot	118
Journey's End	119
Dates in Stone	120
Gullfoss	121
St Martin's, Bulmer	122
The Wards	123
Halloween	124
'The Poet's Wife'	125
The Worsley Arms	126
Bonfire Night	127

References to TH are to Thomas Hardy's 21 elegies for his wife Emma, published as 'Poems of 1912–13' in *Satires of Circumstance, Lyrics and Reveries* (Macmillan, 2014).

Please No

I'mstrugglingtobreathe, pacingtheconfinesofmysmallroomin Canberra, fearingtheworst, butwithnopossiblemeansofknowing thetruthbeforedaybreakonthefarsideoftheworld, whenthecause ofyoursilencewillbediscovered, pacingmyroom, fearingthetruth, knowingtheworst, nomeansofbreathingdaybreakhereonthe wrongsideoftheworld, andallIcanthinkispleaseno, pleaseno, drillingmyselftoacceptwhatmayhavehappened, anditseems there'shardlytimebeforeit'shappeningagain, pacingthehospital carparkasI'mtoldourdaughtermaynotreappear,struggling tograspthatImayneverseeheragain, thoughIdranktoherthirty-fourthbirthdaylastnightinthepub, nothingnowtodobutpace thecarparkforhours, hours, seeminglyforever, withonlywhat passesforprayer, pleaseno, pleaseno, pacingtheconfinesof fear,knowingnopossibleendtothisworldwithoutdaybreak, withoutno, pleaseno, pleaseno, please no

TH: 'The Going'

Our Separate Ways

You drove me to the station as I was leaving for Australia. I'd be back in six months, but as the train pulled out I saw your face through the window, and your tears, which told a different story. I was focused, then, on my adventure, but I think now of your drive home, contending with those tears; fifteen miles – a longer, harder journey than mine around the world. I picture you on the road out of York, at the turning where, nearly thirty years before, you'd made the first of your too generous decisions: to carry on working, leaving me to bring up our baby at home – and to write. I remember my surge of happiness, as you held the wheel around the bend – and my paltry appreciation of what you'd done. I wonder what you did when you returned, that day of my departure, to an empty house, an uprooted future. Now, at least, I know something of how it felt. But I remember, too, how once, in the Louvre, we went our separate ways, wandering in different directions, at different speeds, and how you gleaned from that small sign that we might happily marry.

TH: 'Your Last Drive'

The Steps

A bright wintry day in Washington DC. We'd done the National Gallery of Art, and walked on through Constitution Gardens, seeing our own faces in the polished black granite behind the veterans' names. The sun was threaded into the long Reflecting Pool. A friend took a photo of me staring down into the darkly mirrored sky. Then it was you and me, smiling into camera for the final time. As we reached the steps to the Lincoln Memorial, you stalled. I thought it ridiculous: we'd come this far. I bounded up the steps to see the colossal marble statue, set back behind Athenian columns, staring out to where you were sitting. I didn't know about the atherosclerosis, closing off your heart, didn't know how my trivial irritation would one day turn to anger at my own ignorance. In the intimate Rothko Room of the Phillips Collection, I lost myself in the warm walls of colour, *not memories but old emotions disturbed or resolved—some sense of well being suddenly shadowed by a cloud.*

TH: 'The Walk'

Snow

The whole village is blanketed. I pull on the thick wool jacquard socks, and boots, then tread a soft path to the churchyard, where you're buried, a stone's throw from home. The wind chill is bitter. I won't be able to stay long – a frailty that feels painfully like guilt, but which suddenly dissolves as I think how you're now impervious to the cold: it won't worry you ever again. There – I've managed to turn a fact into fancy. And now you hear the blue snowflakes settle on your grave, our daughter in the adjacent plot listening in. I'm heartened, even while I numb to the point I struggle to move. But move I must – such is the survivor's lot – as the light begins to fail. A dull crunch in each homeward footfall warns me the snow is compacting to ice.

TH: 'Rain on a Grave'

The Submerged Cathedral

When I was a child, I spake as a child, but sang unchildish words as chorister in the cathedral. At the Christmas service of nine lessons and carols, we processed to the west end of the nave, by the tree, where those members of the congregation without seats clustered round. And there you were, as a child, neither of us knowing our proximity. We were as close as we are now – now that I've grown to a man and you lie six feet beneath where I stand. You might so easily have been born in Kenya, Nepal or Singapore, you claimed, rather than the less exotic army base of Aldershot. But you put away that childish pique when you discovered our shared past. We imagined how I might just have brushed against you as I skirted around the tree. I can feel my hand lifting from my side, above your grave, as if you're there still in that ethereal evening submerged in our memories. Perhaps you can hear, like I do, the choristers' voices that still resonate. But touch – touch was always so improbable.

Black Dog

I walk into the Castle Howard Chapel and immediately catch sight of my hangdog expression, as if in a mirror: one of four full-sized video screens – black monoliths from *2001*. Someone complains that they're blocking off the altar, but the prayer box is full like never before. *People We Love*. Mere days after our daughter's death I had volunteered to be filmed while staring at her photo. Why hers not yours? – I asked myself then, as I do now. The slowly moving portraits last a few minutes each, before dissolving, and giving way to a new person. I look more closely at mine, aghast. It's an old grey dishcloth, wrung out. Other faces look more at peace. Some transpose into smiles, as they recall some small happiness, while I remain trapped in haggard gloom, as if willing myself to disappear. I think of your own vanishing acts: storming off to bed, or simply not turning up for a concert, or flight, when the darkness took hold of you, leaving me beside an empty seat. Then you vanished for good – such a ludicrous phrase. I think of Lara's photo, her smile. But I remember her own bleak grief at your going, and her subsequent fury with me. My crime? Not being you. All I could do was bargain for a better version of myself. I look once more at the traumatised flickerings in the fog of my gaze, and think of the photo yet again, your face still visible in hers. All good.

TH: 'Without Ceremony'

Blue Christmas

We would always divide the tasks, though it wasn't a fair bargain: me dealing with the cards, and the tree; you fighting the supermarket crowds, doing all the cooking. I struggle now, trying to follow your example; my penance, knowing how far I fall short. Even in writing cards – my own practised domain – I stumble: such is the muscle memory in my hands – perhaps too the habit of head and heart – that I nearly add your name. Never mind my poor efforts: how you would have loved this last Christmas together with both daughters. And Elvis. The CD sits there, your favourite. It's only a matter of time until one of us will dare play it, and the familiar, mellifluous opening groove pleads with our memories. The notes are the same, but each blue snowflake cradles a different emotion; blue itself now a strange new colour.

TH: 'The Lament'

'Somewhere Only We Know'

I walk down Wandale Lane, that Keane song playing in my head, careful of my footing on the muscular slicks of ice. There's no dog at my side, as once there was, pulling dangerously on the leash; you cast her ashes over the rose bed a decade ago. And though you rarely came with me on this walk – partly for reasons I now know – your greater absence today is an almost palpable accompaniment; unconflicted, neither of us with a grouse, or cause to hurry back. I think I see a hare up ahead, holding stock-still, then turning to race away as if chased by the dog, and skipping sideways through a frosted hedge to where I can't follow. *Oh simple thing, where have you gone?* I retrace my steps up the hill, hand in hand with solitude, towards home.

TH: 'The Haunter'

Your Laugh

was unmistakeable, breaking out of nowhere and rattling through the house. I could hear it from a distant room, through walls almost two feet thick. It seemed to fuel itself to greater velocity, while staying resonant with charm. Once, in the semi-darkness of a long-haul flight, with headphones, watching a comedy, you were blissfully unaware of your outburst startling the whole cabin. We were powerless to stop you – it was too much fun. Infectious laughter, we say, but it's not a disease. If it were, I'd be less troubled now my memory of your laugh begins to fade – not the hilarity so much, just the contours of the sound, as if the word legendary were dwindling away. I have a sense of panic, my stomach clenching as if in turbulence, fearing our plane might fall from the sky. Then the walls of this room re-materialise around me. I catch an echo: laughter in the house again, our two grandsons running riot.

TH: 'The Voice'

Renovation

We did our house up on the cheap. Since you've been gone, I've made some amendments, which I think you would approve: insulating the stone barn walls, so that the wind no longer tunnels through the crumbling mortar; repainting rooms grown shabby with neglect, though I find that task on a list in your handwriting, stuck on the fridge. Other items on the list remain to chide me: *wedding dress, gate hook, shed*. I put it in a drawer. When the fridge packs up, I choose a new one, duck egg blue, utterly different from 'yours'. It's myself I need to please. I don't actually believe you can see any of what I've done, but still I think twice before hanging new paintings, and finally – wanting your impossible blessing – placing a new photo beside my bed.

TH: 'His Visitor'

Autumn Collection

The quotidian junk mail falls through the letterbox to patter on the floor. There are bills, in your name. I begin by feeling cross, but eventually accept it's my fault that I haven't made the change. Is there anything for me? No. Just catalogues from your favoured suppliers. I look through them, imagining it's you, not the range of predictable models, doing the stylish clothes some justice. But the beautiful autumnal tones, in which you'd have looked so good, are simply sad. They go in the bin. And now at last it's time to go through the wardrobe and be ruthless. Every dress in which I remember you so fondly needs a reason to remain. Others I've never previously seen: new purchases for occasions you'd never attend. Might they yet be worn? Lara's clothes have already gone to the charity shop; the charity that saved her life, just for a while.

TH: 'A Circular'

Saint-Juliot

Why go to Saint-Juliot? What's Juliot to me? I'm one step removed from Hardy's tortuous question, never having been there at all. I feel alarmed – as I search the map of our past – that you and I never had a Juliot of our own. I've no such compass point by which to navigate my grief. Yes, it was the west country where we met, but far from any sweep of romantic coast. Instead, the mêlée of your boyfriend's party in the heyday of punk. His parents' house was trashed. Over the years, we recounted the story, perhaps with an eye to some originary mayhem of our love. Yes, our Juliot exists – in all the *flounce flinging mists* of random time and place, and the bittersweet realms where they take us.

Journey's End

It's always death. I knew that, supposedly, travelling back to take care of your funeral, the hardest task of my life. But you were leading me to a further gruelling duty – to take our daughter to the chemotherapy ward for the last of her sessions. We played Scrabble on her iPad; she looked chirpy with the cold cap on her head. The slightly foul smell turned out to be a smear of dogshit on my shoe. Then it was daily radiotherapy in a city some twenty-five miles from home, a trivial distance that quickly became the longest haul. SatNav. Easy! But at the very first roundabout she and I misread the signs, and fell into an all-too-predictable muddle, saddled with blame. We turned it into a companionable ritual, clocking the landmarks that made us smile: *Professional Barber Shop*, *Cash Direct*, and *the friendliest pub in Yorkshire*, which we never managed to pass at an opportune time, to put its claim to the test. I register all of that nonsense again, as I'm taken there by friends for sessions of my own. *Carpets & Households. 2nd Time Round.* I'm appalled, as I sit staring at the familiar treatment room doors, that I might be grieving for myself. Please no. How you would have scorned me for failing to open Lara's bottle of morphine at the requisite speed. I feel my useless fingers still fumbling with the childproof top. Where is there to go from here?

TH: 'After a Journey'

Dates in Stone

On your death certificate there's a date that's wrong, so I believe. It's not your death-day, but the one when we finally knew for sure what we had feared, through who knows how many hours. I was eleven ahead. It was Lara who devised the Bulmer/Canberra clock, an elegant, silvered twin dial for each of us, so that we could keep track of where we were in our disjointed world. The hands crawled round, but only I was looking. A whole year now since you were buried, and still no headstone. I walk to the churchyard to stare at a slightly hollowed patch of grass. As the months go by, I feel an increasing anger at someone not doing their job, not answering calls, emails, not even there whenever I hammer on the door. I cancel, and he suddenly appears at my front door with a bottle of wine. Sorry. It's not good enough. I give the job to someone more efficient. On the day the stone finally arrives, I'm strangely excited, then shocked as I read the chiselled name and dates, all perfectly done, just brutally terminal, no glimmer of doubt.

TH: 'A Death-Day Recalled'

Gullfoss

You stand there in your habitual black, and dark glasses, above the Gullfoss canyon, a tremendous tonnage of green-white ice-water churning below. There's a thin length of safety rope behind you; on one of the poles a small triangular red and yellow sign, with the ubiquitous, cautionary stick man caught flailing in the air as he slips to his fate. I scroll on through the remaining reel of that last trip. No more photos of you, just landscape: fire and ice; endless waterfalls that fail to purge my sense of loss; worse, the sudden beauty of an erupting geyser, a sharp reprise – but of what? They seem worthless, these images. How easily I could go back there, and see the very same, never though with you in the frame.

TH: 'Beeny Cliff'

St Martin's, Bulmer

I walk to the church with our older daughter in her wedding dress, *your* wedding dress, her sister Lara with the other bridesmaids, just behind. You are already there, in our pew. And after I have walked with Anouska on my arm down the aisle, I still don't join you, darting back to the organ to play the first hymn. Three years later, we follow you again, this time walking down the middle of the street, behind the hearse with your coffin. Once more, I go my own separate way, to play you in, then to let my hands do the work through the hymns, rather than trust my fragile voice. The vicar jokes about the trouble I'm in, now he knows I play the organ like that. But he doesn't know the hours I've spent practising – not just until I know the music by heart, but until I can't possibly forget it. He doesn't know I couldn't do it for anyone else. He jokes again – about the two occasions he's seen the church so full, the Mundens to blame both times. It puts everyone at ease. I think, though, of the many other weddings and funerals that have taken place here, and the many more to come. And yes, here I am walking with Anouska down the middle of the street, then the aisle, behind her sister's coffin. And yes, I was right, I can't play the organ again. Not today, though I'll eventually come here on my own, now and then, to sit in the empty church, pull out all the stops and make the stained glass tremble.

TH: 'At Castle Boterel'

The Wards

A second breech baby was an event – trainee doctors and nurses crowding in to witness little Lara's feet-first birth. So slender, she was *off the scale* – the ratio of length to weight. Who remembers that now though, except me? Staff move on; the ward is redeveloped, its whole purpose the future, not the past. But there are those still there today on a different ward, who said they would never forget her, our brave daughter in their care for the two weeks following her final birthday, the sixth that you had missed. I can see the window of her room, high up in the niche between hospital blocks, as I pass on the street. There's someone else in that room of hers now. Yes I know.

Halloween

Our wedding day. It was an innocent mistake. As we left the reception, we were shepherded away from the Bride of Dracula shenanigans kicking off outside the officers' mess. Every year after that, we acknowledged the clash, acquiring a pumpkin, quarrying the pulp and carving a face – each time a new expression flickering into life as we placed a candle in the hollow behind the eyes. When you were no longer with us, I carried on the ritual with our daughters. In the window between lockdowns, our masterpiece sat on the old Remington typewriter, with a shining snarl, a plastic axe in its head. *All work and no play makes Jack a dull boy.* I think of that carefree autumn in Vienna, wondering if I could possibly revisit our haunts, the restaurants and bars, *strung with cobwebs, a pumpkin on every table*, borderland between the living and the dead. Would the phantom be you, or me? On the morning we left, two pale horses in blue raincoats, harnessed for a wedding carriage, stood ready for their task.

'The Poet's Wife'

You planted the aptly named rose beside our front door, where it thrived. Each yellow bloom is a splash of sunshine as I step out into the world. Other whims of your planting are more challenging: roses that rear up like thorn-bedevilled phantoms in the borders; the spiky purple berberis that shreds my gloves, then fingers, as I try to prune it back, year after year. When badgers ransack the lawn, and a conspiracy of moles moves in, I begin to feel victimised; the whole garden a belligerent critique of my domain. But on your birthday, there they are, with their buttery bright petals, the wifely flags of a truce. I cut three blooms to place in a jar on your grave.

TH: 'The Spell of the Rose'

The Worsley Arms

I wake one morning knowing what I must do: revisit the pub where I went on the Saturdays of Lara's hairdresser appointments. Perhaps you went there with her too, while I was away. I would walk around the village, before adjourning to wait for her in the Cricketers' Bar, bedecked with its bizarre memorabilia. I don't for a minute expect the landlord to remember me, or her, but he comes straight towards my table. I'm preparing what I want to say, when a group of tourists comes between us, and he does the proper thing, giving them the time of day, before sending them on their way and turning back to me. By now though I've lost the plot, struggling to tell him about my mission, Lara gone, but he saves me – with his own story of how the hairdresser has shut down. And in that moment the whole room tilts, and I slowly regain my balance. I'd been wrapped in my own grief, adrift from the world.

TH: 'St Launce's Revisited'

Bonfire Night

After poetry and music in the church by the Minster, we cross the road to the Guy Fawkes Inn. I sit with Lara in the small front room – *the same / As when we four came* ... for dinner, some forty years before; four until we married. *Two have wandered far ... And one – has shut her eyes / For evermore.* Pennies on eyelids. Pennies for the Guy – which meant money for fireworks from the local shop. A conflagration, regular as Christmas. I'm still there with my father at the end of the garden, watching him light a Roman candle, or Catherine wheel pinned to a homemade scaffold, my mother holding me back; still there with you and our daughters by a bonfire in the field, our faces alive in the glow against a dark green backdrop of trees. We all whirl sparklers in the air. Burnt gold circles and glittering infinity loops are inscribed on the cold November night, and etched on the inside of our eyelids for when we sleep. You bring us hotdogs, or baked potatoes in silver foil. In the morning, the fire is mostly gone, but the scorched earth remains.

TH: 'Where the Picnic Was'

Notes

Sources of italicised quotations and other references within the poems are as follows:

3. Duncan Phillips, 1964. https://www.phillipscollection.org/press/phillips-collection-announces-unprecedented-reinstallation-its-renowned-rothko-room
4. Elvis Presley, 'Blue Christmas', on *Christmas Peace*, CD, RCA/BMG, 2003
5. Paul's first letter to the Corinthians, 13.11
6. *People We Love*, multi-screen video installation by Kit Monkman, 2020 onwards (touring). https://www.kma.co.uk/people-we-love
7. See 4.
8. Keane, *Hopes and Fears*, CD, Interscope records, 2004
12. Thomas Hardy, 'A Dream or No', in 'Poems of 1912–13'
13. Various signs in Harehills, Leeds
18. First quotation from *The Shining*, dir. Kubrick, 1980; second quotation from Paul Munden, poem 7 from *The Music Lovers*, Authorised Theft, 2020
21. Thomas Hardy, 'After the Picnic', in 'Poems of 1912–13'

INDIVIDUAL POETS' STATEMENTS

PAUL HETHERINGTON

John Fowles writes, 'The Greece of the islands is Circe still; no place for the artist-voyager to linger long, if he cares for his soul' (2004: 9). These islands are also places of real magic: a quotidian, blood-tugging mystery, that seems to rise from the rock and tough foliage. These places were, strangely and impressively, the source for a great deal of what used to be called 'Western' culture, which now might simply be referred to as ancient Greek civilisation – although the ancient Greeks were never one people.

To stand in the scarifying light of a summer's day on one of the Greek islands can be to realise that the reflective self and the world are deeply implicated in one another, and often uncomfortably and sadly so. The sun, the landscape and the ocean seem to speak at once of ambition, desire, grief, and the pervasive, expressive, inarticulate presence of loss.

This statement may appear fanciful. Yet others have written of such emotions and apprehensions, including John Fowles in his introduction to his novel, *The Magus* (1965). Fowles says he wanted in that work 'to provide an experience beyond the literary' (2004: 6) and partly drew on his reading of Alain-Fournier's extraordinary, searching, wanting novel, *Le Grand Meaulnes* (1913) in order to do so. Fowles also talks of 'deeper biographical influences' (7) related to his experiences on the island he calls Spetsai (Spetses), which partly relate to his sense of what the place connoted and suggested beyond the rational:

> Away from its inhabited corner Spetsai was truly haunted, though by subtler – and more beautiful – ghosts than those I have created. Its pine-forest silences were uncanny,

unlike those I have experienced anywhere else; like an eternally blank page waiting for a note or a word. They gave the most curious sense of timelessness and of incipient myth. In no place was it less likely that something would happen; yet somehow happening lay always poised. The *genius loci* was very similar indeed to that of Mallarmé's finest poems of the unseen flight, of words defeated before the inexpressible. (8)

The inexpressible is partly what much captivating poetry is about as it searches the ineffable yet powerfully visceral terrain of cognition and emotion. Additionally, the recognition of loss and grief that a certain quality of light may provoke and even examine – and which may possess an uncanny sense of waiting, too – is well suited to poetry's quest to locate, and try to name, some of the unspeakable things.

These issues inform my sequence, *Aegean Blues*, as it looks toward beautiful and uncanny shifting registers of island light.

Works cited

Fowles, John 2004 [1965] *The Magus*, London: Vintage

OZ HARDWICK

Uncharacteristically, I didn't know where to start with this. Usually, I can come up with an author statement or accompanying commentary, no problem, and it's something that I enjoy doing. But this time, in the push and pull of approach to, and avoidance of, grief, the poems themselves mark a threshold beyond which I don't wish to pass.[1]

As Inge B. Corless et al. point out in their overview of the key features of the expressions of grief, symbolism and metaphor – specifically *personal* symbolism and metaphor – play important roles in what they describe as an individual's 'articulation not only of loss but potentially of gain, growth, and the birth pangs of a new personal synthesis,'[2] and I worry that if I lay bare the symbolism and metaphor of my poems, I might undo the latter part of these workings. Indeed, I don't even want to put into plain words the specific loss which prompted these responses, and will instead just note that it was neither the loss of my parents nor the loss of myself.

I didn't lose my parents until I was in my 50s. They had long, full lives, and we were very close. I still miss them, and grief remains a constant though managed presence. I lost myself a little later, with an autism diagnosis that, along with understanding and relief, brought the realisation that I had never been who I had been

---

[1] Eisma, Maarten C, & Lonneke IM Lenferink, 2023 'Co-occurrence of Approach and Avoidance in Prolonged Grief: a Latent Class Analysis', *European Journal of Psychotraumatology* 14, 1-12

[2] Corless, Inge B, et al. 2014 'Languages of Grief: a Model for Understanding the Expressions of the Bereaved', *Health Psychology and Behavioural Medicine* 2, 132-43 (132)

pressed into thinking I was. I don't miss the lost self that much, yet, as I was warned may be the case in my assessment debrief, it has left a grief that I am still processing, and quite possibly always will be. But, as I said, neither of these is at the diamond-hard core of these poems, and I mention them purely to avoid a subject to which I don't want to lean in too close.

In fact, rather than addressing that which I'd rather not speak of, I'm inclined to write about Hawkwind, the space rock legends who have provided the soundtrack – and so much more – to my life for well over half a century.[3] It's a topic upon which I can enthuse endlessly, in the inimitable manner of any autistic individual on one of their monotropic obsessions. There is, for me, nothing to beat the disorienting rush of light and sound of a Hawkwind gig, and the way it envelops me entirely and sweeps me away from everything unmanageable in the day-to-day – including, of course, grief.

But then, in the midst of the throbbing riffs and electronic squawks and squeals, there's one of their often-overlooked interludes, coruscating with stoned nostalgia for lost innocence – a thematic commonplace of British psychedelia, as much as a 'generalised elegiac mode' is a thematic commonplace of contemporary British poetry[4] – plaintively evoking the transience of perfect beauty which, on reflection, may never have really been there at all. And with this comes grief, that 'houseguest that arrives without invitation': because music that has provided succour and respite throughout my life has also, of course, been grief's constant companion.[5] So I remember, after my mother's death, clearing out the house in which I was born and grew up: the house where I'd first seen Hawkwind on the little black and

---

[3] For a visual representation thereof, see Martin Popoff, *Hawkwind: A Visual Biography* (Wymer Publishing, 2021), in which around 250 of my photographs are reproduced.
[4] Kennedy, David 2007 *Elegy*, London & New York: Routledge, 127
[5] Moules, Nancy J, et al. 2004 'Making Room for Grief: Walking Backwards and Living Forward', *Nursing Inquiry* 11, 99-107 (104)

white TV in the living room, and where I'd listened over and over again to their first dozen or so albums in my bedroom. And here I was, taking down the framed Hawkwind posters Mum and Dad had hung in the hall, so alien to their tastes, but proudly displayed because they featured my photographs.

As I think about this, I welcome grief as the houseguest to which I've become accustomed, 'expected at times, its comings and goings not surprises, its intrusions not unanticipated.'[6] This time, though, it's not alone, and there's a young woman, too, who previously only ever visited the house and met my parents on one occasion, and who once came to see Hawkwind with me in a functional provincial theatre about 40 years before she died.

Now, she's walking along the corridor and down the stairs, and although I was nervous of welcoming her back after all this time, it's good to see her in these poems.

---

[6] Ibid.

CASSANDRA ATHERTON

La petite mort, or 'the little death', is an idiom for an orgasm. While it was first used in 1572 to define a fainting fit, and later used to describe a nervous spasm, it wasn't until 1882 that it became associated with women's pleasure. The connection with death is symbolically associated with the loss of consciousness that can accompany an orgasm, or deep, post-orgasmic sleep.

Aristotle believed too many orgasms were harmful for men because they depleted their life force, while Bataille's 'La Pratique de la joie devant la mort' ('The Practice of Joy before Death') explores *la petite mort* as a transgression of individual boundaries. Furthermore, in *The Pleasure of the Text*, Barthes' connects *la petite mort* to *jouissance* or the bliss in reading and losing yourself in a good book. More recently the little death has become popularised by Taylor Swift's lyric, 'I died the tiniest death', and possibly the small batch wine range, 'La Petite Mort', which focuses on the joy of drinking good wine.

My poetry sequence draws on the work of two important poets, Nin Andrews and Victoria Chang. Nin Andrews is known colloquially as Queen of the Orgasm for her extensive poetry oeuvre on orgasms, including *The Book of Orgasms*; *Our Lady of the Orgasm*; and *The Last Orgasm*. Here, she acknowledges *la petite mort* in 'I Do Not Know French, *after Michael Palmer's "I Do Not"*':

> I do not know French.
>
> Though I have tried to learn it, to decipher it word by word, letter by letter, and accent grave by accent aigu by accent circumflex – but the cedilla is the one I like best. And yet I do not know French, and everyone knows the orgasm

only speaks French and always prefers an o who has been circumflexed.

[...]

Nor do I know what the orgasm means when she sings. Or if the names she calls me are insults or compliments. Names like *Sacrebleu*, *Mon Dieu* and *Zut Alors*. And if this sadness I feel when she leaves is hers? Or mine? Or yours? And if I should ask.

[...]

Oh my Love, I do not know French. (2018: n.p.)

Andrews' prose poem personifies the orgasm as French or a Francophile, referencing the phrase *la petite mort*. The orgasm teases the narrator with its elusiveness and tortures her with post-coital *tristesse*. This is a clever rebuttal of Greek physician Galen who said in 150 CE that every animal experiences sadness after coitus, except the human female and the rooster. The orgasms in Andrews' poem are lost in translation.

My second reference is to Victoria Chang's *Obit: Poems*. Chang's book of prose poems is set out as obituary columns and explores her father's death from a stroke and her mother's death from pulmonary fibrosis. This leads to Chang charting her own metaphorical deaths in four separate obituaries, including:

> Victoria Chang – died unknowingly on June 24, 2009 on the I-405 freeway. Born in the Motor City, it is fitting she died on a freeway. When her mother called about her father's heart attack, she was living an indented life, a swallow that didn't dip. This was not her first death. All her deaths had creases except this one [...] (2020: 7)

Chang also eulogises the death of many other things, writing obituaries for 'Secrets', 'The Blue Dress', and in an important nod to the Kantian sublime, 'Language' dies twice. Finally, Chang writes an obituary for 'Grief':

> Grief – as I knew it, died many times. It died trying to reunite with other lesser deaths.
>
> [...]
>
> If you cut out a rectangle of a perfectly blue sky, no clouds, no wind, no birds, frame it with a blue frame, place it faceup on the floor of an empty museum with an open atrium to the sky, that is grief.   (2020: 70)

My prose poetry sequence explores twenty-one little deaths (*la petite mort*), or female orgasms, as obituaries. In this way, it construes the little deaths as actual deaths. The prose poem is the perfect form for this suite as their fully justified boxes of text are visually akin to columns in the newspaper, specifically obituaries. The sequence also critiques the slang term, box, for female genitalia. This critique is elaborated on by Holly Iglesias in *Boxing Inside the Box: Women's Prose Poetry*.

    Like Chang, I use my own name and the date and place where these orgasms supposedly occurred to build tension, but also to discuss the loss of self. Chang's obituaries mourn a breakdown in language and the ineffability of death. Extending these ideas, I suggest the little deaths when we orgasm are sublime – drawing specifically on Lyotard's notion of the postmodern sublime and the limits of language.

    This sequence does not take the topic of grief lightly. It simply aims to channel grief into a feminist form of gallows humor, as a coping mechanism. I also hope this sequence which plays on the 'O' of Obituary with the 'O' of Orgasm also gives more visibility to the female orgasm and pleasure.

Works cited

Andrews, Nin 2018 'I Do Not Know French', *DMQ Review*, Winter, https://www.dmqreview.com/andrews-winter-2018

Barthes, Roland 1976 *The Pleasure of the Text* (trans Richard Miller; with a note on the text by Richard Howard), London: Jonathan Cape

Bataille, Georges 1985 'La Pratique de la joie devant la mort' ('The Practice of Joy before Death') in *Visions of Excess: Selected Writings, 1927–1939* (ed. Allan Stoekl), Minneapolis, MN: University of Minnesota Press, 235-9

Chang, Victoria 2020 *Obit: Poems*, Port Townsend, WA: Copper Canyon Press

Iglesias, Holly 2004 *Boxing Inside the Box: Women's Prose Poetry*, Williamsburg, MA: Quale Press

La Petite Mort Wine: https://bentroad.com.au/#labels

Swift, Taylor 2024 'I Look in People's Windows', *The Tortured Poets Department*

JEN WEBB

This topic seems to have been nosing around us, we five thieves, for some years, as though looking for a gap it might fill. When Paul Munden proposed the five stages of grief as our next – our tenth – annual collection, it stopped us in our tracks. We let a whole year go by until someone suggested that rather than each of us taking on one of the stages, we would simply write to all of them.

The concept of the five stages – denial, anger, bargaining, depression, acceptance – is outdated, though of course is still cited in much of the literature on grief. Current thinking is that each stage does operates, but not as part of a linear process where the stages are worked through, in order, and then put aside. They co-exist, and they persist. We are tumbled between and across them, as though in a high sea, coming up now and then for breath before we are rolled again.

Like most people, I have a fairly close relationship with grief, having been brought into contact, as a young child, with the character whom EE Cummings (cuttingly? bitterly?) calls 'Mister Death', and with Death's reality, its finality.

Its finality? Yes; in a manner of speaking. Mourning, writes Françoise Dastur, is a matter of 'coming to terms with absence' (2015: 8). Yet 'the dead haunt the living' (Certeau 1986: 3); we re-experience deaths we have attempted to forget; we write in ways that afford opportunities to create presence in absence; or at least the idea of presence, the sense that I have sensed my lost loves, albeit briefly. We write in the attempt to 'work through', to keep present what has been lost, to keep the faith, to maintain memories, to figure out how we can continue living and creating and being reasonably sane in the face of grief. And, perhaps, to begin coming to terms with our own inevitable death, Larkin's 'small unfocused blur'. Or to accept grief, as Denise Levertov does when she proposes, in her 'Talking to Grief', that she will 'trust' Grief, 'give you / your own corner'; because grief is always with us, 'like a homeless dog' who should be recognised, and accommodated.

I don't know that I could actually 'coax you / into the house'; but I do think that, as humans among humans and other living beings, it is a good idea to recognise rather than wrestle with grief. Certainly I have been reading poems about death, grief and mourning for most of my life, and writing a fair number of bleak pieces myself. The poems I have included here are my small effort to accommodate myself to grief / grief to me. I'd intended to organise them in clusters, each set addressing one of the five stages of grief, but the engine of narrative trumped that idea, so instead these 21 prose poems are organised in terms of different kinds of grieving: anticipatory mourning; sorrow; denial; a hint of anger; a kind of acceptance. No bargaining, not even in anticipation. All but two are accounts of griefs I have personally experienced; the other two are griefs I have observed in those who are close to me. And while I know that grief is the product of a wide range of losses, in these poems I have focused on what I think of as capital-G Grief: the grief occasioned by the death of those we love.

Works cited

Cummings, EE 1991 '[Buffalo Bill's]', in *Complete Poems: 1904–1962* (ed. George J Firmage), New York, NY: Liveright, 90

Dastur, Françoise 2015 'Mourning as the Origin of Humanity', *Mosaic: A journal for the interdisciplinary study of literature* 48.3: 1-13, https://doi.org/10.1353/mos.2015.0037

Hughes, Langston 1984 'Island', in *Selected Poems of Langston Hughes*, New York, NY: Vintage Books, 78

Larkin, Philip 1988 'Aubade' in *Collected Poems*, London: Faber & Faber, 208-09

Levertov, Denise 1978 'Talking to Grief', in *Life in the Forest*, Cambridge, MA: New Directions, 43

PAUL MUNDEN

My part in this Authorised Theft project owes everything to my seemingly random decision, just over a decade ago, to take up a position at the University of Canberra. It was a short-term post, during which time my family remained in England. The rewards for me a writer were immense, but the adventure also put me at a remove from those whose health would suddenly fail. My wife Clare died in 2017; our younger daughter, Lara, developed the breast cancer that would eventually kill her in 2023.

 As I embarked on these poems, I happened to be re-reading the poems Thomas Hardy wrote after the death of his wife Emma, the 'Poems of 1912–13'. I was intrigued to find that these elegies – in the final form that we know them – number 21, the very same number of poems we task ourselves to contribute to these Authorised Theft anthologies. We 'thieves' have license to borrow from each other's work. In this instance I decided to go further, and borrow from Hardy too. Hardy and his wife had become totally estranged. My own situation was different, but the geographical remove was nevertheless significant. Perhaps more importantly, the focus of Hardy's individual poems seemed – uncannily – a match for those I had in mind. I have detailed the match at the end of each poem; my titles are different but the sequencing remains Hardy's.

 It was harder by far to match the poems to the so-called five stages of grief, but I did make sure that I dwelt on each of them to some degree, though not necessarily in the notional order; and sometimes two or more are entwined (as with Hardy). My biggest issue was with the terminology of the stages. Words, after all, are crucial here, and though 'depression' and 'acceptance' seem accurate enough, I struggle with the other three. 'Denial' for me is all wrong: 'incomprehension' or 'disbelief' might be closer to the mark. 'Anger' might loom large in the case of a hit-and run, but I've mainly directed it against myself. 'Bargaining' seems plain weird, though I have of course felt 'if only'; does that count? But where is the sheer *distress*, the *devastation, loneliness, fear*? I guess that's why we have poetry. Having said which...

I read many collections of elegies in preparation for this project, and amongst the high-profile offerings were some that left me cold (it would be churlish to name them). One that I found immensely moving, however, was Adrian Caesar's book, *This Cathedral Grief*. It helped me unlock the route to scrupulous, raw honesty, as did Claudia Emerson's collection, *Late Wife*. Betty Adcock, endorsing Emerson's book, makes reference to the 'sparer diction' adopted for the task. I found myself similarly drawn to a very direct form of expression, believing that strong emotion needs no elaboration. I pulled back from too much metaphor, also of course the short-lined, rhyming structures that characterise most of my poems, this being a prose poetry project. I am not, primarily, a 'prose poet', but I have undertaken each of our shared prose poetry anthologies with a deep commitment not only to the chosen theme but also the experiment with form. In this case, the claustrophobic box seemed a perfect fit for the approach I wanted to take – at a deliberate remove from Hardy's elaborate and intricate verse.

I set out to write poems about losing Clare; I felt that Lara's death was too recent to contend with in poetry. But just as one funeral we attend brings memories of others, writing about one bereavement inevitably pulled me towards the other; they were mother and daughter, after all.

Works cited

Emerson, Claudia 2005 *Late Wife*, Baton Rouge, LA: Louisiana State University Press

Caesar, Adrian 2020 *This Cathedral Grief*, Recent Work Press

Hardy, Thomas 1914 'Poems of 1912–13', in *Satires of Circumstance, Lyrics and Reveries*, London: Macmillan

ABOUT THE POETS

Cassandra Atherton is an award-winning and widely anthologised prose poet, a leading international scholar of prose poetry and Distinguished Professor of Writing and Literature at Deakin University. Her books of prose poetry include *Exhumed* (2016), *Trace* (2016), *Pre-Raphaelite* (2018), *Leftovers* (2020) and the forthcoming *Short Poems* (Life Before Man, 2025). She is currently writing a book of prose poetry on the atomic bomb. Her scholarly and edited books include, with Paul Hetherington, the authoritative monograph *Prose Poetry: An Introduction* (Princeton UP, 2020) and the *Anthology of Australian Prose Poetry* (Melbourne UP, 2020). With Paul, she is currently writing *Ekphrastic Poetry: An Introduction* (Princeton UP, forthcoming). Cassandra is dispatches editor of *The Fortnightly Review*, associate editor at MadHat Press (USA) and commissioning editor for *Westerly* magazine.

Oz Hardwick is a poet, photographer, music journalist, and academic, whose work has been widely published in international journals and anthologies. He has published 'maybe fifteen?' solo full collections and chapbooks, most recently *Retrofuturism for the Dispossessed* (Hedgehog Poetry Press, 2024), along with several collaborative collections with other poets. Oz has won several prizes: some for poetry, others for pub quizzes and hooking fairground ducks. His compulsive creative endeavours are both symptom of, and coping mechanism for, his autism, and his recent academic work – the logic-defying hybridity of which resembles a medieval grotesque as animated by Victor Frankenstein – explores this relationship between neurodiversity and creativity. At time of writing, Oz is Professor of Creative Writing at Leeds Trinity University.

Paul Hetherington has published 18 full-length collections of poetry, most recently *Sleeplessness* (Pierian Springs Press, 2023) and *Ragged Disclosures* (Recent Work Press, 2022), along with a verse novel and 14 chapbooks. His work has received more than 50 awards and nominations, including the inaugural The Marion Halligan Award (2024) for *Sleeplessness* and the 2021 Bruce Dawe National Poetry Prize. With Cassandra Atherton he co-authored *Prose Poetry: An Introduction* (Princeton UP, 2020), and co-edited *Ricochet: An Anthology of Microlit* (Spineless Wonders, 2025) and the *Anthology of Australian Prose Poetry* (Melbourne UP, 2020). He is Emeritus Professor of Writing at the University of Canberra and founded International Poetry Studies (IPSI) in the Centre for Creative and Cultural Research there. He is also a founding editor of the international online journal, *Axon: Creative Explorations*.

Paul Munden is a poet, editor and screenwriter living in North Yorkshire. He was director of the UK's National Association of Writers in Education for nearly 25 years, and more recently a Royal Literary Fund Fellow at the University of Leeds. He lived in Australia for several years, running Poetry on the Move, the festival initiated by the University of Canberra, to which he remains affiliated as an Adjunct Associate Professor. He has published seven poetry collections, including *Amplitude* (Recent Work Press, 2022), and *Peckinpah Suite* (RWP, 2025), a sequence focused on the legendary American film director. He is also the author of *Unclassified: Nigel Kennedy in Chapters & Verse*, a study of the maverick violinist. He is currently working on a film based on Thomas Hardy and his elegies of 1912–13. https://paulmunden.com

Jen Webb is Distinguished Professor Emerita of Creative Practice at the University of Canberra, and a poet who writes (mostly) prose poems. Her most recent book is *The Daily News* (Recent Work Press, 2024). Other poetry publications include *Watching*

the World (with Paul Hetherington, 2015), *Sentences from the Archive* (2016), *Moving Targets* (2018) and, with Shé Hawke, *Flight Mode* (2020). With Kavita Nandan she edited the anthology *Writing the Pacific* (2007); with Paul Hetherington she produced the Mandarin/English poetry anthology *Open Windows: Contemporary Australian Poetry* (2015); and with Monica Carroll she published the collection of interviews, *Everyday Words & Creative Practice: Ten Australian Poets in Conversation* (2019). She is co-editor of the literary journal *Meniscus* and the scholarly journal *Axon: Creative Explorations*.

IPSI: INTERNATIONAL POETRY STUDIES

The International Poetry Studies (IPSI) was established in late 2012, and was one of the four pillars of the emerging Centre for Creative and Cultural Research in the Faculty of Arts and Design, University of Canberra. Between 2013 and 2023 IPSI conducted research related to poetry, publishing and promulgating the outcomes of this research internationally. It also published poetry and interviews with poets, as well as related material, from around the world. Publication of such material took place in CCCR's online journal *Axon: Creative Explorations* (www.axonjournal.com.au) and through other publishing vehicles. IPSI's goals included working – collaboratively, where possible – for the appreciation and understanding of poetry, poetic language and the cultural and social significance of poetry. Though IPSI has been disestablished, much of its work continues in the CCCR under the twin pillars of Arts & Health and Creative Sustainable Communities.

CCCR: CENTRE FOR CREATIVE AND CULTURAL RESEARCH

The Centre for Creative and Cultural Research (CCCR) is IPSI's umbrella organisation and brings together staff, adjuncts, research students and visiting fellows who work on key challenges within the cultural sector and creative field. A central feature of its research concerns the effects of digitisation and globalisation on cultural producers, whether individuals, communities or organisations.